Upgrading Leadership's Crystal Ball

Five Reasons Why Forecasting
Must Replace Predicting and
How to Make the Strategic Change
in Business and Public Policy

Upgrading Leadership's Crystal Ball

Five Reasons Why Forecasting Must Replace Predicting and How to Make the Strategic Change in Business and Public Policy

JEFFREY C. BAUER, PhD

Foreword by Dr. Stan Gryskiewicz,
author of *Positive Turbulence*

CRC Press
Taylor & Francis Group
Boca Raton   London   New York

CRC Press is an imprint of the
Taylor & Francis Group, an **informa** business

A PRODUCTIVITY PRESS BOOK

CRC Press
Taylor & Francis Group
6000 Broken Sound Parkway NW, Suite 300
Boca Raton, FL 33487-2742

© 2014 by Taylor & Francis Group, LLC
CRC Press is an imprint of Taylor & Francis Group, an Informa business

No claim to original U.S. Government works

Printed on acid-free paper
Version Date: 20130925

International Standard Book Number-13: 978-1-4665-5403-0 (Paperback)

Library of Congress Cataloging-in-Publication Data

Bauer, Jeffrey C.
   Upgrading leadership's crystal ball : five reasons why forecasting must replace predicting and how to make the strategic change in business and public policy / Jeffrey C. Bauer.
      pages cm
   Includes bibliographical references and index.
   ISBN 978-1-4665-5403-0
   1. Business forecasting. 2. Economic forecasting. 3. Strategic planning. I. Title.

HD30.27.B38 2014
330.01'12--dc23   2013023916

Visit the Taylor & Francis Web site at
http://www.taylorandfrancis.com

and the CRC Press Web site at
http://www.crcpress.com

Dedicated to leaders with the courage to look beyond
current trends to the realm of future possibilities

Contents

Foreword

Thank you, Jeff Bauer, for writing this superb guide to a process that today's creative leaders can use to prepare their organizations for success in rapidly changing environments. As promised in its title, the book provides an essential update of ways leaders can look at the future. By applying the tools of forecasting, rather than predicting, healthy organizations will have the ability to renew themselves continuously and thrive under conditions of uncertainty. Jeff's refreshing new focus on assessing the probabilities of possibilities will allow public and private enterprises to use turbulence as a catalyst for strategic innovation—for managing change before change manages them. He gives us a better road map that can be used with any strategic planning model to anticipate and shape appropriate responses to change.

More than ten years ago, my own work identified the positive value of using turbulence from the periphery to disturb the status quo in which organizations and their leaders usually operate.* They may have been successful in the short haul, but they operated at their ultimate peril by not considering and adjusting to alternative futures. Turbulence represented the winds of change that would influence their system. My question was, why not manage that process proactively for better

---

* *Positive Turbulence: Developing Climates for Creativity, Innovation and Renewal,* by Stanley Gryskiewicz, San Francisco: Jossey-Bass. 1999.

outcomes? Hence, I developed the concept of *positive turbulence* to describe a culture that values and seeks this external novelty. The core concepts in Jeff's new book mesh perfectly with the implications of my earlier work—as reflected in the common references to weather phenomena.

Where in the past most leaders saw turbulence as a threat, Jeff's forecasting model helps them to see turbulence as a whirlwind of options for change, renewal, and ultimate success—options that they can evaluate and assign a probability. Creative organization leaders who scan the periphery for transformative forces can respond with ideas and processes to solve the complex problems associated with change; in this way, they create the meaning and set the tenor for a culture that is compatible with different futures. This approach illustrates the enduring wisdom of something once said by Dee Hock, founder and CEO emeritus of Visa International: "Residing on the periphery of the organization today are the ideas which will revolutionize the organization tomorrow."

Although it is operationally sound to focus daily tactics on organizational maintenance from an internal perspective, the most vexing challenges to survival will come from outside the organization. Yes, there have always been external challenges and changes, but now that we operate in a global context and a wired world, they come more frequently from more exotic and surprising sources. If leaders are unaware of these forces, or fail to understand them, they have little or no control over the direction in which change pushes their organizations. Here again, Jeff's powerful distinction between predicting and forecasting gives structure to my earlier thinking and provides creative leaders with a new tool attuned to the 21st century, one that allows them to assess and ultimately manage changing environments in ways not previously recognized as possible.

I would be remiss if I did not deliver a riff on innovation to explain what is happening here. There is a theme that emerges when stories about innovation are told: again and again, an expert in one field (in Jeff Bauer's case, meteorology) brings a way of thinking that provides breakthrough innovation in a second (health care). This theme runs through the stories of how General Motors found ideas at Tiffany's when it needed a more efficient way to paint automobiles... how Hallmark sent staff to TED conferences for new product ideas... how an Ohio hospital hired an administrator from the hotel industry to improve its patients' experiences... how scientists at Bell Labs after hearing an expert on whale communication speak developed a better way for submarines on patrol to communicate. (To prove the point, it should be noted that the expert on whale communication first trained as an ornithologist.) You are in good company, Jeff!

To honor Jeff's succinct and very readable work, I am keeping my word count low, but my praise is high for this very practical process for forecasting the direction of future change. His book provides creative, visionary leaders with the concepts they need to make smart decisions and informed choices. In Jeff's own words, "The future has many possibilities." His process will help leaders identify these possibilities from the periphery, bring them inside, and assign them meaning for directing organizational change, renewal, and ultimately its survival. By complementing their experience and knowledge of their fields with the images and ideas from an updated crystal ball, leaders now have what it takes to, as Henry David Thoreau said, "go out and build foundations under them." Thoreau, Henry D. *Walden; or Life in the Woods* (Boston: Ticknor and Fields, 1854).

Stanley S. Gryskiewicz, Ph.D.
Chairman & Founder
Association for Managers of Innovation
and Senior Fellow, Creativity and Innovation
Center for Creative Leadership

Chapter 1

Introduction

Forecasting is about **predicting** the future as accurately as possible.

—**Rob J. Hyndman,**
***Business Forecasting Methods* (2009)**

Forecasting is a strategy used in different fields to **predict** the future based upon the past.

—**Forecastingmethods.net (2013)**

An economic **forecast** is a **prediction** of what future periods of economic activity will be in various categories.

—**Investment Contrarians, February 26, 2013**

Economists are **forecasting** the same steady, if unspectacular, growth this year they were expecting in 2012. Last year's **predictions** proved too optimistic.

—***Wall Street Journal,* February 8, 2013, p. A2**

There is nothing immediately jarring about these top-ranked responses to a Google search for "predicting + forecasting." We would expect to find many sentences containing both words because they mean exactly the same thing, right? Wrong.

A typical prediction would posit a year-end annual economic growth rate of 3.5% for 2013. On the other hand, a true forecast would estimate something like a 25% chance of economic decline, a 40% chance of no growth, and a 35% chance of increasing growth between 2012 and 2013. These two statements do not have the same meaning. They represent very different outlooks on the future and call for different approaches to it.

The common practice of using *predicting* and *forecasting* as synonyms is dangerous and needs to stop. Both terms identify well-accepted methods for looking ahead in a variety of domains, but the similarity stops there. Simply treating them as different words to describe a single prognostic process robs us of the power to envision and pursue good outcomes, especially when we are headed in bad directions. The resulting semantic imprecision compromises our futures.

We will be better off when decision makers realize that there is more than one way to look into the crystal ball, our most common metaphor for formal efforts to see where we may be headed. Those of us who base our actions on what we expect in the future have a surprising consequential choice to make. As you will see in the following pages, progress will be more likely when we deliberately decide to forecast—not predict—the futures of a wide variety of dynamic systems in both public and private sectors.

This book is a practical guide for understanding highly significant, poorly understood differences between predicting and forecasting. It lays out compelling reasons why forecasting is more appropriate for the twenty-first century. Because transcendent forces are redefining futures globally, the content that follows is applicable in any line of business.

New Definitions

Given the dominance of predictive approaches to futurism in the twentieth century, our long-standing lack of concern about significant operational differences between predicting and forecasting is understandable. Indeed, the two words are defined identically in the authoritative *Merriam-Webster Dictionary*:

> **predicting** *noun* a declaration that something will happen in the future

> **forecasting** *noun* a declaration that something will happen in the future

Merriam-Webster is not making an etymological error. Its lexicographers are ably performing their role of capturing and explaining common usage. The problem is the common usage, not the dictionary's definitions. Those who want a generic term that encompasses *prediction* and *forecast* can use *projection*.

After initially defining a prediction and a forecast as the same thing, Wikipedia introduces an important nuance in its discussion of these two parallel processes for "making statements about events whose outcomes (typically) have not yet been observed."

> A **prediction** (Latin *præ-*, "before," and *dicere*, "to say") or forecast is a statement about the way things will happen in the future, often but not always based on experience or knowledge. While there is much overlap between *prediction* and *forecast*, a *prediction* may be a statement that some outcome is expected, while a *forecast* is more specific, and may cover a range of possible outcomes.

Recognizing any difference between a prediction and a forecast is a move in the right direction. However, for reasons that will be made obvious in the following chapters, the Wikipedia entry is still insufficient and imprecise. (To set the record straight, a prediction is statistically more specific, but a forecast's range of possible outcomes is more practically useful.)

Here are my "new-and-improved" definitions, crafted to differentiate two well-established approaches to foretelling events that have not yet happened:

Prediction: a specific estimate of the expected value of a key variable at a future point in time

Forecast: an estimate of the probabilities of the possibilities for a key variable at a future point in time

Because a prediction and a forecast are different concepts, predicting and forecasting are correspondingly different methods for producing them. Vive la difference. In particular, note the singularity of a prediction and the plurality of a forecast. We will all benefit when those responsible for shaping our future understand this distinction and use the right tool for anticipatory decision making. For a variety of reasons explained in the following pages, forecasting is the better tool for the unpredictable future that we all face.

The Difference Matters: Chance and Uncertainty

Why should you care enough about such a seemingly trivial point to spend a few hours reading a book about it? Understanding the predicting-forecasting difference and putting it into practice could greatly increase your chances for success or, at the very least, keep you from making avoidable mistakes.

And, why do I care enough to spend nearly a year writing the book? By pure happenstance, I have been formally trained in both predictive and forecasting sciences—economics and meteorology—and have come to understand the distinction between them over a 40-year career as a medical economist and health futurist. In this book, I distill what I have learned into some innovative principles that can be applied to create better futures in any industry or public service organization.

I stress the role of chance (quite frankly, good luck) in my two-track professional formation. Life, as they say, is what happens when you are making other plans. Neither path was an intentional choice; I wanted to become a diplomat or politician when I was growing up. The unanticipated educational paths were set before me as the result of two earthshaking events during my high school and college years: the space race and the Vietnam War. Fortunately, you do not need to have shared my experiences as a student in the sixties to understand why I believe forecasting is the better way to approach the future in today's literally unpredictable world. I have structured this book to provide the necessary knowledge transfer without subjecting you to vicarious time travel.

My forecasting studies began in 1964 when I received a National Science Foundation grant to do research at the National Center for Atmospheric Research (NCAR) in Boulder, Colorado. The project sought to explain the formation of hailstones and to develop interventions for reducing hail's economic damage. I was trained to forecast storms so that research teams could be sent into the field to collect data when and where hail was most likely to fall. Project Hailswath and subsequent work in applied forecasting kept me very busy for 6 years (and resulted in my first professional publication, an article for the *Journal of Atmospheric Physics*).

NCAR's concern with the costs and benefits of deploying expensive field research teams under conditions of uncertainty, plus my sixties era angst about being socially relevant, led me to change my undergraduate major to business and economics in my senior year. I ultimately completed a PhD in the "dismal science" of economics—a discipline firmly focused on making predictions. However, I never lost interest in forecasting during my ensuing career as a medical economist. By the mid-1980s, I took on another role, health futurist, and I have spent the past 25 years working to influence health reform with forecasts rather than predictions. I have also maintained my general interest in forecasting methodologies by reading about their specific applications in other fields.

Hence, I have written—and you are reading—this book because the superiority of forecasting in our turbulent times extends far beyond the medical marketplace. Problems in any industry are much more likely to be solved over time when leaders purposefully shift their future views from data-driven extrapolations of historical experience (predictions) to open-minded assessments of the realm of future possibilities (forecasts). Reading this book should make you a better manager of the resources you control in any line of work, public or private. It will change the way you look into your crystal ball.

The Content to Come

To establish an appropriate context for understanding predictive science's declining relevance to steering an enterprise, Chapter 2, "Predicting," begins with a review of the nonscientific methods—including crystal ball gazing—that constitute the historical foundations for telling what and when something will happen in the future. Enlightenment era foundations of predictive sciences are then described in the context of the ongoing human quest to build mathematical and statistical models that explain how systems work and where they are headed. The enabling power of automated data processing receives special attention in the context of computers' impact on the evolution of social sciences and public policy studies. Finally, the scientific theory and practice of predicting are explained and illustrated with real-world examples of the interplay between predictions and managerial decision making in a variety of sectors.

Chapter 3, "Five Fatal Flaws of Predicting," shows why the basic methods of predictive science—in spite of their expanding use over the past 50 years—are now generally inappropriate for looking even 5 years into the future of most dynamic systems. The discussion identifies serious inconsistencies between the theoretical assumptions of predictive modeling and the real world in which the models are applied, and it exposes related problems created by deficiencies in available data. As proof of decision makers' need for a better way to gain business insight, the chapter notes predicting's long, sad history of failures and raises serious concerns about things becoming even worse as organizations increase their reliance on quantitative analysis to chart their future course.

Chapter 4, "Forecasting," explains how forecasting—predicting's lesser-known fraternal twin—is methodologically consistent with the increasing uncertainty that obscures our views of better futures and ways to create them. It presents a step-by-step overview of weather forecasting and shows why the meteorological model has so much to offer as a crystal ball prototype for other dynamic systems. The chapter highlights underlying assumptions that differentiate forecasting from predicting and explains why public and private enterprises should use forecasts as the foundation for decisions that will shape their futures in unpredictably better ways. Steps for evaluating the accuracy of forecasts and evaluating the impact of climate change are also included.

Chapter 5, "Forecasting in Dynamic Systems," presents a "how-to" guide for making forecasts in business, government, and other dynamic systems in which predictions are bound to fail. It describes key steps in the process and relates them to uncertain futures in the public and private sectors. Ultimately, it gives you, the business decision maker, a process for looking into your own crystal ball under conditions of uncertainty, with insight into the realm of possibilities and actions that you can take to produce a better future by managing alternatives—creatively, constructively, and productively. The chapter also reflects on the difference between art and science and emphasizes the importance of finding the right balance between humans and computers in a world increasingly addicted to data.

Chapter 6, "From Forecasts to Strategies," explains the powerful link between forecasting and strategy. Starting with updated definitions of strategy and strategic planning, the chapter shows how predicting's rise to power since the 1970s has caused business and government leaders to forget strategy's real meaning and its creative applications. The practical importance of time frames for business decision making is also explained. Finally, the chapter presents specific steps that you can take to enhance your chances for success by using a forecast-based strategic planning process attuned to the uncertainties of today's dynamic systems.

Postscript, "Big Data," ends the book with a general analysis of big data's suitability as a futurist's tool and a specific forecast of its future. The relevance of predictive analytics over time is examined from both perspectives, suggesting that big data has much to offer but is unlikely to be the next crystal ball. However, it can survive on its own substantial merits if emerging problems are appropriately addressed.

The Less-Is-More Approach

"If you can't explain it simply, you don't understand it well enough."

Albert Einstein

A funny thing happened as I began writing this book. It grew much shorter than the 300-page volume originally proposed to the publisher. I quickly realized that organizational leaders who need to understand forecasting do not have time to become experts in it. They need to know why they should base strategic decisions on forecasts rather than predictions, and they need to know how to get and use good forecasts. Staff and consultants can do the follow-up work of looking into the upgraded crystal ball.

Consequently, I took the extra time to write a shorter book—fighting every author's natural inclination to provide too much information (TMI), which ultimately obscures a book's take-home lessons. Readers who feel the need for more detail can consult the references presented at the end of each chapter or conduct online searches based on individual interests. This book will accomplish its goal if, after reading it, you, the decision maker, agree with my initial premise that the common tendency to use predicting and forecasting as synonyms must end *and* know how to select and apply the right tools for looking strategically at the future in your very own dynamic system.

Citing Precedent

I believe I am on solid ground and in good company when promoting definitional correctness. *Upgrading Leadership's Crystal Ball* is not the first book to argue that business opportunities are lost when executives fail to operationalize significant differences in words erroneously used as synonyms. In one of the all-time business classics, *Management: Tasks, Responsibilities, Practices* (New York: HarperCollins, 1973), Peter Drucker showed how a company's long-term performance can be explained by how well its managers differentiate two concepts, marketing and selling, which are usually used interchangeably.

In Drucker's formulation, marketing is a coordinated set of ongoing activities to understand the whole business from the customer's point of view. It permeates the seller's enterprise, resulting in product innovation that meets buyers' changing needs and contributes to their success. Marketing enhances economic progress. It is an engine of creative destruction, a core strength of our economic system eloquently described by Joseph Schumpeter in *Capitalism, Socialism, and Democracy* (New York: Harper and Brothers, 1942). In contrast, selling is the practice of trying to convince customers that they need the seller's existing product. Selling leads to commoditization and stagnation, not growth and renewal.

The stunning decline of the American automobile industry during the 1980s and 1990s illustrates how serious problems can be created by decision makers' failure to respect differences between key management concepts—like sales and marketing or predicting and forecasting. Based on impressive sales gains during the 1970s, the Big Three automobile manufacturers predicted consistent growth, and they continued selling cars with the same old value propositions. American automakers did not use forecasting to explore future probabilities of different possibilities created by rising energy prices, declining family sizes, changing lifestyles, and increasing acceptance of globalism. They paid no attention to consumers' evolving needs and expectations. Prediction-based selling led Detroit to a debacle that could have been avoided by forecast-based marketing.

On the other hand, foreign manufacturers listened to American consumers and respected their new preferences by producing smaller, sportier, fuel-efficient, low-maintenance cars. Toyota, Honda, Volkswagen, and other outsiders looked at the future as a realm of different automotive possibilities and made strategic plans accordingly. The rest is history.

American investors, workers, and taxpayers have paid a very high price over the past two decades because a leading industry's executives failed to grasp the differences in two key business concepts. In contrast, North America's leading high-tech companies understood the differences precisely and became very successful.

Acknowledgments

If this book is successful, it reflects the quality of instruction I received from my meteorological mentors at the National Center for Atmospheric Research and from my economics professors at Colorado College and the University of Colorado at Boulder. I have been predicting and forecasting long enough that almost all my teachers are retired, and several are deceased, but I honor their commitment to good teaching. This book would not have been possible without the following atmospheric scientists who so generously introduced me to the fundamentals of meteorology: Guy Goyer, Sonia Gitlin, Ottavio Vittori, Tarani Bhadra, Robert Bushnell, Myron Plooster, Nancy and Charles Knight, Walter Orr Roberts, Richard Schleusner, Alex Koscielski, Helmut Weickmann, Jan Roszinski, John Marwitz, and Augie Auer. I am also happy to recognize the contributions of my main mentors in economics: Ray O. Werner, Michael Bird, Larry Singell, Wes Yordon, Vince Snowberger, Barry Poulson, and especially Kenneth Boulding.

I express appreciation to good friends who responded so generously to requests for help in updating my knowledge in some key areas and commenting on the manuscript: Allen I. Goldberg, Jean-Pierre Thierry, Thomas Hay Bauer, Douglas Parker, Gerard Nussbaum, Chris Barker, Stan Gryskiewicz, Brian McDowell, Amy Rohling McGee, Marc Ringel, Hunt Kooiker, Kenneth Cunningham, Aissa Khelifa, James Heckman, Gayle Morse, and Gilbert Johns.

Extra appreciation is owed to Dr. Adam French, a specialist in meteorology and severe storm forecasting at the South Dakota School of Mines and Technology in Rapid City. I approached Dr. French because he now teaches the forecasting courses at the university where I learned about weather back in the 1960s. His thorough professional review and constructive comments were extraordinarily helpful throughout all stages of this book's evolution. He could not have done a better job providing me with resources to update my knowledge of forecasting techniques. Of course, I wrote all this book's explanations of forecasting, so I am solely responsible for any errors.

Special recognition also goes to Lauren Phillips, my professional editor. She is a superb wordsmith and insightful idea checker. This book has benefitted enormously from her attention to clarity, especially her help with turning professional jargon into practical, meaningful text and developing real-world examples.

The contributions of my editor at Taylor & Francis, Kristine Rynne Mednansky, must be mentioned. I couldn't ask for a better professional partner in making sure that my proposal and manuscript ultimately turn into a published work. This is the seventh book Kris and I have done together (with an eighth under contract), proof of her remarkable skills in managing the complex interface between writer and reader.

Finally, I cannot say enough to thank my wife, Beth, for putting up with me and keeping life in order while I was once again in "book-writing mode." I also thank the kids—Anna, Frank, and Chuck Bauer and Parrish Steinbrecher—for their continual reminders to avoid TMI. Enough said … let us start by putting predicting in perspective.

Example 1.1: The Difference between a Prediction and a Forecast

The *Wall Street Journal* is an excellent source of experts' predictions. Editor Michael Hickins reported a textbook example in his *CIO Journal* blog on March 25, 2013. SWIFT, an interbank transactions network that processes five billion transactions a year, announced its analysis of these data by predicting that the European recession of the early 2000s would end with a +0.4% gross domestic product (GDP) growth rate (the expected future value of a key variable) in the first quarter of 2013 (the future point in time). According to SWIFT's head of pricing and analytics, the prediction is based on a technique that outperforms other economic indicators because it uses real transactional data in near real time.

Not surprisingly, and illustrating this book's key premise of the need for forecasting, SWIFT's prediction did not evaluate or even present other possibilities. On the same day, other media reports discussed several forces that could cause the European recession to continue: bank closures in Cyprus, a decline in the euro, higher-than-expected budget deficits in several key European Union countries, a freak winter storm that closed businesses across the continent, inability to reach expected budget deals in France and Italy, and growing rejection of bailouts by Germany. None of these current determinants of economic activity was reflected in the historic transactions data that generated the prediction.

In contrast to the SWIFT prediction, a forecast of Europe's economic future would reflect the bigger picture, with estimates of probabilities of all the possibilities: decline, stability, and growth (for illustrative purposes, say a 50% chance of continuing recession, 30% of stability, and 20% of growth). The forecast would be a much more realistic and useful tool for decision making because it incorporates multiple factors that make the future of Europe's economy literally unpredictable. Economic activity everywhere is likely to go in several different directions, and no expert can say for sure—a compelling reason for making the strategic shift from predicting to forecasting. (By the way, the European growth rate at the end of the first quarter was not the +0.4% predicted by SWIFT, but −0.9%, as reported in a front-page story in the *Wall Street Journal* on May 16, 2013.)

Chapter 2

Predicting

Introduction

Professionals have been in the business of making predictions for thousands of years. Historical records show that seers in northern Europe had their own tools of the trade as early as the third millennium BCE. For example, druids used Stonehenge and other rock alignments to predict coming changes in the seasons. Fortunately, their use of ritual human sacrifices to influence the future has not survived in modern practice.

Their counterparts along the Mediterranean exposed older women "of blameless life" to fumes escaping from the cracks in the earth at Delphi. Once intoxicated, the oracles presumably communicated with the gods and uttered random sounds that priests then translated into insights about the future. Unfortunately, the pretense of having unique powers to turn unintelligible information into useful insight for public consumption has survived to the present day—a major reason for this book.

Development of the Western calendar is likewise early evidence of a professional class dedicated to predicting: A systematic list of days and months gave Roman philosophers an unprecedented capability to assign a specific date to a future event. The time-sensitive warning to Julius Caesar, "Beware the Ides of March," is probably one of the most widely recognized examples of foretelling an event and suggesting an anticipatory response. At roughly the same time in Central America, the Mayans had temples to translate the "language of the skies" *and* a calendar that foretold events—including the end of the world, which we have now safely passed.

The Emblematic Crystal Ball

Today's prevailing image of a tool for looking into the future is the crystal ball. Crystal ball gazing (originally called scrying) is more socially acceptable than forcing slaves to transport large rocks or drugging intermediaries to induce hallucinations, and it is has not caused wars over the interpretation of prophecies based on religious convictions. Although the geographic origin of scrying—gleaning a picture from an inanimate object—is not known, the practice is described in the histories of several ancient cultures.

Ironically, the classic study on the topic, *Crystal Gazing: Its History and Practice, with a Discussion of the Evidence for Telepathic Scrying*, by Northcote W. Thomas (New York: Dodge, 1905), discredits the idea of being able to see the future in a crystal ball, a glass of water, a mirror, or any other reflective medium. Thomas's extensive research found credible examples of people using crystal balls telepathically to find lost objects and to describe current events that were happening at a distance. However, in studying fortune-tellers around the world and over the centuries, he could not find believable evidence that anyone had consistently used a crystal ball to describe future events with accuracy any greater than random chance.

Given the absence of any contradictory scientific studies in the century since the publication of Thomas's book, fortune-tellers with crystal balls are still very much on the fringes of respectable futurism. The occasional political candidate or business leader who admits having consulted with a crystal ball gazer is not taken seriously, if not openly ridiculed. The financial press puts more credence in dart throwers as a control group when testing the accuracy of investment advisers' stock picks for the coming year.

"Sometimes the future is bright, sometimes it's dark—it's all cyclical."

Nevertheless, gazing into a crystal ball survives as the prevailing metaphor for efforts to foretell what will happen. Journalists almost always refer to the practice when writing about the future, and cartoonists frequently use it in their work. (I will bet that a crystal ball appears in more *New Yorker* cartoons than any other inanimate object. I thank *The New Yorker* for permission to use a representative sample of these cartoons.) Pictorial and verbal images of exploring the future with a crystal ball are universally understood, making the tool an appropriate emblem for this book. I actually keep a crystal ball on my desk, but like a lawyer who displays a balance to symbolize justice, I never use it for anything more than symbolic inspiration.

Scientific Foundations of Predicting and Modeling

Additional anecdotes from the history of predicting are available for the interested, but they will not help today's leaders select the best way to look ahead and prepare their organizations for the future. The past and present are worlds apart in terms of criteria used to evaluate the unknown future. With the exception of celestial observatories made from aligned rocks, the old tools for making predictions did not have any research or systematized knowledge behind them; their origins were spiritual or supernatural, not scientific.

Of course, discrediting several millennia of futurism on modern scientific grounds is unfair because modern science is relatively new. Greek and Roman philosophers of the Classic period (e.g., Aristotle, Pythagoras, Heraclitus) developed subjective, rational methods to analyze natural events that could be observed with the naked eye, but objective science and supportive technology to help us understand measured

"Something goes around something, but that's as far as I've got."

dynamic processes—major forces that shape the future—
began to emerge only a few hundred years ago.

Predictive science was born in 1687 with *Mathematical
Principles of Natural Philosophy*, Sir Isaac Newton's treatise on
formulas for converting historical data on physical objects' tra-
jectories through space and time into their positions at specific
points in the future. Newton's revolutionary work effectively
established the concept of *modeling*, the use of mathematical

equations to represent how a system works and to predict how it will evolve over time. Newton did conceptually with math what priests had done physically with stone temples. For the first time, scientists had a methodological tool to discern patterns hidden in data.

Newton's laws of motion systematized a mechanistic view of natural forces that worked in precise, consistent ways. This underlying assumption of a "clockwork" universe was *the* foundation of scientific thought for more than 200 years. The orrery, a device that looked like a clock, was constructed to demonstrate the universe's mechanistic precision. Following the publication of *Principles*, mathematicians began discovering and refining formulas for making predictions based on the assumption that the natural order of things can be meaningfully represented by mathematical laws and equations. Dozens of such formulas accumulated since Newton are the conceptual building blocks of models that experts still use to predict the future.

Appropriate Uses of Predicting

The development of applied mathematics since Newton is fascinating to explore, but executives do not need to know much about this history to be competent, future-focused decision makers. The one point they must understand is the pivotal role that consistency plays in the theory and practice of traditional predictive sciences: Useful predictions can be made when the quantifiable relationships that represented how things worked in the past will continue to work the same way in the future.

If you can defensibly make this assumption about the marketplace or other sphere in which your enterprise operates, you can confidently use predictions as part of your decision-making process. Predictions are perfectly appropriate for analyzing future states in historically stable systems that are expected to remain stable for the projected period of time, assuming good data and good methodological practices. Common violations of these preconditions are discussed in the next chapter.

Note that I am not arguing that predicting is intrinsically wrong and always to be avoided. Predictive models are perfectly rational when the same variables and relationships that adequately explained the past can reasonably be expected to explain the future. I simply cannot think of very many, if any, dynamic systems for which this is the case today. The growing problems of using the past as a precursor are also addressed thoroughly in the next chapter.

To paraphrase George Santayana's famous observation in the context of today's unsettled dynamics, understanding the lessons of history is no longer enough to avoid doom in

"Those who do not learn from the future are destined to make mistakes in it."

the future. We cannot possibly have learned lessons about many key determinants of our futures because we have not yet experienced them. Today's decision makers are entering unfamiliar territory, and they need navigational skills that are embedded in the art of forecasting, not in the science of predicting. Nevertheless, because stability is still possible in some systems, it is important to understand predictive science. In the increasingly rare circumstances for which historical relationships are not expected to change, a prediction can be a valuable aid in preparing for the future.

Statistical Foundations of Predicting

Once predicting's mathematical foundations were laid in the late eighteenth century, its applications throughout the nineteenth century were devoted almost entirely to understanding the natural world. Development of reliable instruments of measurement (microscopes, scales, rulers) enabled the collection of calibrated data that scientists could analyze mathematically to explain and predict workings of the physical universe. In this way, the modern foundations of basic science (chemistry, physics, biology) grew apace throughout the nineteenth century, making the Industrial Revolution possible and reinforcing the mechanistic worldview.

Systematic efforts to explain and predict events outside the realm of nature did not start until the late nineteenth century, when governments began collecting extensive data on human populations, economic activity, and social characteristics that could not be measured with a physical device. Proliferation of handwritten data in public records ultimately created a new problem—too much information for bureaucrats to analyze. Collecting numbers was easy, but processing them was a cumbersome, time-consuming process done by hand. (Younger readers may be surprised to learn that almost all data analysis was done with pencil, paper, a mechanical adding machine, and a slide rule until introduction of electronic calculators in the early 1970s.)

Because governments could not handle all the demographic data they were collecting in the late nineteenth and early twentieth centuries, it was necessary to invent statistical analysis—a body of theoretical constructs for using samples to describe large sets of data and to infer population parameters. (Indeed, the word *statistics* is derived from *state*, as in the nation-state as a data unit.) Unlike Newton's eighteenth century scientific formulas, which were direct mathematical expressions of physical laws, statistical formulas were derived from assumptions about the mathematical characteristics of uniform, randomly drawn samples of full population data. In other words, statistics developed as a shortcut for understanding large databases without actually looking at all the numbers.

Statistics developed without the rigorous proof and experimental verification that underpin the laws of thermodynamics or the periodic table of elements. Where Newtonian mechanics can define the future position of an object moving in space with verifiable certainty, statistical analysis can only make inferences, that is, arrive at a probability (the p value) that an outcome is explained solely by chance—the luck of the draw inherent in random sampling. By definition, projections based on statistical analysis are uncertain. Anyone who uses statistics to plan for the future must remember that the resulting prediction is only an inferential estimate, a limitation discussed in the next chapter.

Econometrics and Modeling

Several early twentieth century economists expanded the scope of statistical analysis beyond summarizing demographic data to identifying trends in business activity. For example, in 1910 a Ukrainian bank comptroller named Pawel Ciompa coined the term *econometrics* to describe his new process for using bookkeeping data to project trends in worker productivity. In 1914, Henry Ludwell Moore used time series analysis of historical rainfall records and crop yields to predict future agricultural output in *Economic Cycles: Their Law and Causes* (New York: Macmillan).

During the 1920s, Ragnar Frisch and colleagues published several works on the use of probabilistic techniques to estimate future values of key economic variables. Econometrics ultimately became the generic term for this new field of study. Jan Tinbergen, a Dutch physicist turned economist, was simultaneously applying the principles of cosmological modeling to government economic policy in the Netherlands. Their respective efforts laid the foundations of predictive modeling, for which Frisch and Tinbergen were recognized as joint recipients of the 1969 Nobel Prize in Economic Sciences. In *Economics: An Introductory Analysis* (New York: McGraw-Hill, 1948), Paul Samuelson's justly famous textbook that crystallized economic theory for the next generation, econometrics was lauded for giving economists the capability "to sift through mountains of data to extract simple relationships."

By the 1930s, most economists were conducting at least some empirical analysis to complement their traditional work on theories to explain economic behavior. By the time I completed a PhD in economics in the mid-1970s, statistics and applied mathematics dominated the profession; graduate students of my era had to take at least as many courses in quantitative methods as in economic theory. Our older professors tended to lament the shift, preferring Adam Smith to John Maynard Keynes, but predictive science had unquestionably moved from the periphery to the core of economic science between the 1930s and the 1960s. Thanks to the rapid proliferation of computers in the 1960s, economists

"Tonight, we're going to let the statistics speak for themselves."

finally had the data-processing power to use models in everyday practice.

A *model* is a coherent set of mathematical equations formulated to simulate the inner workings of a system. The science of model building is specifying a set of equations that accurately represents how a system has worked in the past; the art is finding the minimum number of variables and equations that adequately describes dynamics within the system. Once a "best-fit" model has been found through trial runs with historical data, computer simulations can then predict a system's future state(s) by extrapolating the established mathematical relationships to impute new values over time. The metaphorical power of a crystal ball is thus made available to anyone with a computer, data, and a model.

Growth of Modeling

Private and public sector applications of modeling got a real boost in 1972 from an international best seller, *The Limits to Growth* (by D.H. Meadows, D.L. Meadows, J. Randers, and W.W. Behrens III. New York: New American Library). Commissioned by a think tank of European business leaders known as the Club of Rome and written by prominent systems scientists from the Massachusetts Institute of Technology, the book included a detailed description of future-focused modeling. Its conclusions about limits on economic growth were controversial, but the well-written explanations of its methodology introduced many leaders in business and government to the concepts of predictive science.

In line with my previous statement that a model is inherently uncertain due to its statistical foundations (i.e., the probabilistic use of sample data to estimate population parameters), *The Limits to Growth* noted that a model is "imperfect, oversimplified, and unfinished." Models can always be improved with a little manipulation here and there, even in the unlikely situation of an unstable modeled system. Predictive modeling is a good method for looking ahead under the right circumstances, assuming that the model builder is constantly seeking to redefine its variables and formulas. (The process of selecting a model's variables and equations is called *specification*.)

Economists do not have a monopoly on predictive modeling. The multidisciplinary team that wrote *The Limits to Growth* included experts from several academic disciplines. Indeed, the mathematical and statistical techniques of trend analysis are essentially the same in all fields that make predictions, even though nomenclature occasionally differs. However, if you are someone who makes future-focused decisions for an organization, it is important to know that the general term, *predicting*, is used to describe several different approaches: If you have seen one method of predicting, you have seen one method of predicting.

For example, regression analysis is a generic method for making a prediction, but methodologists have developed many ways to do it (e.g., ordinary least squares regression, logistic regression, Bayesian regression). Differences in the computational approaches of each technique will lead to different projections based on the same set of data. Unscrupulous analysts will even try different regression methods until they find one that predicts a future they want to promote. Decision makers should be correspondingly wary of any prediction made by someone who might benefit from responses to it. Failure to understand this point lies behind some of the biggest financial disasters when economic bubbles burst, such as the collapse of the housing market in 2008.

Univariate Predictive Models

The future value of a single variable is generally predicted by extrapolating its historical path into the future. The concept behind univariate predicting is simple: Values of the variable are graphed over time (with time conventionally on the horizontal axis because it is not a variable). An analyst visually—and, one hopes, scrupulously—examines the scatter plot and determines the mathematical form most closely represented by the data points over time, such as a straight line, an exponentially increasing or decreasing curve, or a cyclical wave. A specialized computer program is then selected to run the data according to the designated mathematical relationship and to compute future values that best fit the historical trend.

The problem is that unless the variable's historical values fall exactly on the selected equation's straight or curved line—a *very* rare occurrence—the predicted future values are estimates at best. And, the estimates are meaningful only to the extent that the causal relationships from the past will be the same for the duration of the future under consideration. Univariate predictions are extremely common and tend to be taken seriously, especially when made by people who have a lot of experience with the history of the variable. However, the credibility of univariate predictions is highly suspect in today's dynamic systems, in which almost every relationship is redefined by forces that are unfamiliar even to the experts.

An example from my field, medical economics, illustrates the concept and problems of using univariate analysis to say what will happen and when. To launch the Obama administration's push for a health reform law in 2009, government analysts predicted that health care would consume 20% of the gross domestic product (GDP; the *what*) in 2015 (the *when*). This prediction was intended to force legislators into action on the grounds that it threatened economic recovery from the recession of 2008. Pro-reform politicians wanted to legislate programs that would prevent the cost curve from growing beyond the predicted level.

This prediction is graphically illustrated in Figure 2.1. Between 1995 and 2009, the diamonds that rise vertically across the middle of the graph strongly suggest a linear relationship. (The values for 1980 and 1990 are misleading and should be ignored because they are not on the same scale as the rest of the numbers.) Therefore, a model incorporating the familiar formula for a straight line, $y = mx + b$, was used to compute predicted values for future years through 2015. If the analysts' underlying assumption of a consistent linear relationship is valid and all other things remain equal, decision makers could reasonably believe that the medical sector would consume 20% of GDP in 2015 and act accordingly.

However, as is increasingly the case in the world around us, all other things have not been equal since 2009. The great recession has gone global and lasted far beyond its predicted

**National Health Expenditures and Their
Share of Gross Domestic Product (GDP), 1980-2015**

*National health spending is projected to continue to increase as a
share of GDP over the next decade.*

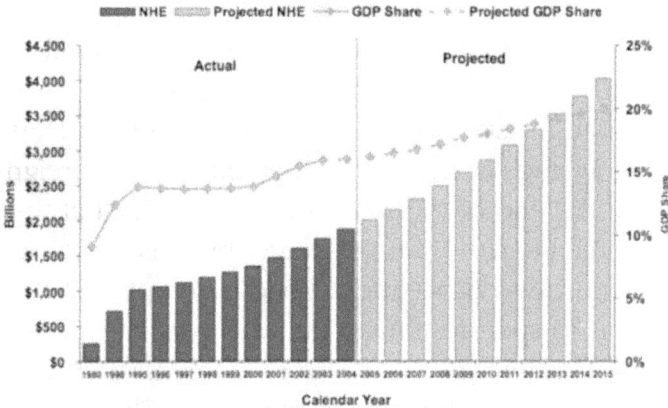

Source: CMS, Office of the Actuary, National Health Statistics Group.

**Figure 2.1   (From CMS, Office of the Actuary, National Health
Statistics Group.)**

end in 2012, which in turn has caused governments and
employers to make unprecedented cuts in planned spending
on health care. Responsibility for payment has been shifted
to consumers, but they have absolutely no available income
to make up the difference. Hence, the assumption behind the
prediction was wrong. (I am making this point to discredit the
prediction and its underlying theory, not the Obama administration; Republicans based their alternative reform proposals
on the same flawed prediction.)

The increase in health spending has fallen well below
expected levels over the intervening years. The medical
economy is actually positioned to experience zero growth by
2015 if the new marketplace forces continue to prevail. If the
medical economy is 20% of GDP in 2015, it will almost certainly be because GDP has fallen proportionally more than
health spending. In my opinion, market analysts are making

a big mistake when they advise investors that health care will continue to be a growth sector—again, based on the original prediction. I currently forecast a 75% probability that health care spending will show no growth in 2015.

Univariate time series analysis of the type behind health reform is particularly common for economic data (e.g., the unemployment rate for the next month, the value of the Dow Jones Industrial Average at the end of the quarter, the foreign exchange rate at the end of the year, the federal deficit at the end of a presidential term). Investors wager billions of dollars every day in response to news about trend-based predictions and pay big sums to specialists who pull the trends from their crystal balls. I am betting the return on investment (ROI) on money paid for such predictions is negative. (See Chapter 3 for further explanation.)

Multivariate Predictive Models

Univariate analysis is simple. It is also simplistic. Given that the only constant is change, future values of any variable are ipso facto explained by something other than the passage of time. Stability may prevail for a while, but not for the long run. (Indeed, the economic definition of *long run* is the time frame within which all factors are variable.) Time alone explains nothing. For example, the exchange rate between two currencies a year from now will be affected by the volume of foreign trade, government economic policies, consumer spending, international relations, Mother Nature, transportation costs, and other factors that vary from market to market and country to country—and not at the same time. No organizational decision maker can know next year's exchange rate with certainty, but multivariate predictive models use historical data to estimate it. The pages of business publications include these predictions every day.

Good multivariate modeling begins with careful review of historical relationships between a dependent variable of interest to decision makers (say, sales of previously owned homes) and two or more independent variables to which the dependent variable is related (such as monthly rent for single-family dwellings and net family income). The relationships can then be expressed in a variety of statistical formulations (with the caveat that correlation between the variables does not imply causality). Each computational approach has its own set of theoretical assumptions and its own adherents. Books and articles that explain the conceptual details of a model are full of equations and functional notations that are incomprehensible to anyone who does not have advanced training in statistics—ample reason to be suspicious of the resulting predictions.

Statisticians love to debate how well different models approximate the complexity of dynamic systems they represent. Comparing computational models is a common project for PhD students in statistics. However, decision makers do not need to understand the debates or the doctoral dissertations. They do need to understand what the very existence of the debates teaches us: There is no single, absolutely correct way to look into a crystal ball. Anyone who claims to have the one demonstrably true predictive model—a perfect representation of reality—is a charlatan.

Regression Equations

Multivariate models are constructed with a string of mathematical expressions that represent the hypothesized relationships between one dependent variable and another variable associated with changes in the dependent variable. Each of the explanatory variables is further assumed to be independent of all the other explanatory variables (i.e., changes in one independent variable have no impact on the other independent variables). A computer program then runs the data to explore how the dependent variable changes with changes in the values of each independent variable while all the other independent variables are held constant.

The net result is a regression equation that expresses the direction (positive or negative) and the magnitude of each independent relationship. Here is the general form of the multiple regression equation:

$$Y = \beta_1 X_1 + \beta_2 X_2 + \beta_3 X_3 + \dots + \beta_n X_n + e$$

Unfortunately, multivariate models cannot be graphically displayed in two dimensions on the printed page because they are, well, multidimensional. The computations are intuitively obvious to anyone who understands matrix algebra but totally unnecessary for you, the organization leader, to know. You only need to know when the models should and should not be used for making predictions that will potentially influence a business decision.

That being said, there is no need to take the time to understand details of analytical techniques from the natural sciences that are ill suited in most other environments. There is considerable value, on the other hand, in knowing why predictions should be met with skepticism in business, government, and other domains encompassed by the social sciences—the topic of the next chapter.

"According to an article in the upcoming issue of 'The New England Journal of Medicine,' all your fears are well founded."

Additional Readings

For accessible discussions of the history of statistics, see Porter, Theodore M., *The Rise of Statistical Thinking: 1820–1900* (Princeton, NJ: Princeton University Press, 1986); and Stigler, Stephen M., *The History of Statistics: The Measurement of Uncertainty before 1900* (Cambridge, MA: Belknap Press of Harvard University Press, 1986). Together, these books provide an essential foundation for understanding the original purpose and limitations of statistical analysis.

The specific statistical concepts introduced in this chapter are explained in plain, nonmathematical English in Bauer, Jeffrey C., *Statistical Analysis for Decision-Makers in Health Care: Understanding and Evaluating Critical Information in Changing Times*, 2nd edition (New York: Taylor and Francis, 2009). Although the book's illustrative examples are drawn from health care, its explanations of basic principles are relevant to any field in which statistical analysis is applied.

An excellent introduction to the role of randomness and applied probabilities is presented in Mlodinow, Leonard, *The Drunkard's Walk: How Randomness Rules Our Lives* (New York: Vintage Books, 2008). A physicist, Mlodinow ably debunks the implications of certainty implied in predictions and provides useful detail about the evolution of worldviews on order and chaos surrounding the time of Newton.

Living the Sky: The Cosmos of the American Indian (Boston: Houghton Mifflin, 1984) by Ray A. Williamson is a great book for anyone interested in the early history of celestial observations in North America. It weaves an entertaining and educational story from archaeological studies of the American Southwest.

Chapter 3

Five Fatal Flaws
of Predicting

Introduction

Predictive modeling has become so common since the 1970s that we do not really think about it. In any realm where data have been collected, predictions have followed. Computer programs that make predictions will analyze any set of numbers. The required software is web-based and often embedded in our operating systems. Consequently, computers handle the mathematical complexities of trend extrapolation with lightning speed at near-zero marginal costs. Search engines lead us to more predictions than we can possibly use. We can even make predictions from our own spreadsheets at the push of a button—not to mention all the predictions that are pushed to us every day via e-mail and the media.

Proliferating predictions can lull us into a false sense of security. It is easy to assume the experts who make them know what they are doing. Predictive science could not have withstood the tests of time if it were not built on solid ground, right? To the limited extent that we think about the current practice of predicting, we probably think our challenge is deciding which predictions to believe. We are much more likely to judge analysts' predictions based on how often they have been right in the past than on careful evaluation of the methodologies they use. A predictor's batting average of career hits *and misses* would be helpful, but I am not aware of any mechanism to hold someone accountable for failed predictions.

Futurists' track records can be very misleading in the absence of accountability. Someone who makes a few lucky guesses can appear to be a crystal ball genius, even though the person was acting on pure intuition or indulging in economic opportunism by telling people what they wanted to hear. A self-fulfilling prophecy can appear in retrospect to be the result of informed judgment, and a cleverly or ambiguously worded prediction can be given the aura of accuracy through "clarification" after the fact. Correct predictions by themselves clearly do not validate predictive science—especially in the absence of counterbalancing information about errors.

However, the question of an individual predictor's success over time fails to address a more fundamental issue: Should we be asking instead whether to believe any predictions at all? Is predicting as currently practiced really any better at foretelling the future than the flip of a coin, the luck of the draw, or a silly wild ass guess (SWAG)? Despite this chapter's title, my answer is not a categorical, "No." Useful predictions are possible. After all, predictive science is based on a solid set of assumptions and mathematical operations. Predictions are also perfectly defensible if the assumptions are valid (e.g., the laws of physics and chemistry), the scientific and statistical methods are properly followed, and the appropriate level of confidence is clearly stated, as is generally the case in physical sciences and engineering.

On the other hand, the conditions that support predicting are almost never met in today's economic marketplaces, government branches, social circles, and other systems driven by human behavior, where any similarity between predictions and the future is likely coincidental. This chapter focuses on five reasons for avoiding predictions in socioeconomic and political domains:

1. Discontinuities in system dynamics
2. Violations of model assumptions
3. Deficiencies of available data
4. Failures of previous predictions
5. Diversions from strategic innovation

1. Discontinuities in System Dynamics

Leaders can make better decisions regarding the future if they have a good sense of what is likely to happen in their *system*—the interacting set of individuals, organizations, economic resources, and circumstances that ultimately define what happens. Invoking systems theory may seem unnecessarily academic, but its practical relevance is evident in our everyday references to the banking system, the political system, the legal system, the educational system, the transportation system, the health care system, the manufacturing system, and so on. All other things being equal, leaders in any system have risen to decision-making roles due to years of experience with its dynamics. They know how things work over time in financial institutions, elected bodies, courts, schools, manufacturing plants, media empires, and so on.

Leaders also know that the future of their own system depends to varying degrees on what happens with related systems. However, they are generally less familiar with the dynamics of the other systems, so they seek predictions from experts in the other systems, such as when a mutual fund manager researches publications of an established oil industry

expert before deciding how much money to invest in petroleum stocks.

People who make predictions that include a specific system
often have no experience working in it. Professional prediction
makers tend to be data geeks who know how to find patterns
in historical data and extend discernible trends into the future.
Knowing how to look at numbers is more important to them
than understanding what the numbers actually measure. For
example, I doubt that experts known for their baseball predictions ever played the game beyond Little League. (In their
defense, becoming either a jock or a geek takes an incredible
amount of time and effort, beginning at a young age. Being
really good at both is probably impossible.) A physician does
not need to have had a disease to predict its course, just as
a rocket scientist can define the trajectory of a space vehicle
without having been an astronaut.

In other words, firsthand experience within a system is
arguably unnecessary for predicting its future if the system's
dynamics are consistent over time. All that is necessary is a
keen ability to find the repeating pattern in historical data and
the mathematical relationship that best represents that pattern.
As already shown in Chapter 2, the theoretical justification
for making predictions since the time of Sir Isaac Newton is
ongoing consistency in system dynamics—the assumption that
how things worked in the past is the way they will continue to
work in the future.

If dynamics change, predictions are correspondingly weakened. The greater the change in a system's inner workings, the
flimsier the prediction—until the new pattern becomes so appar-
ent that the past is no longer an extension of the future. We are
now at this point in the early twenty-first century. Predictions
in almost all our systems are useless, no matter how good the
historical data or how experienced the analyst, because system
dynamics are not what they used to be. And, because anything
not worth doing is not worth doing well, decision makers should

instead approach the future with forecasts, for reasons explained in the remaining chapters of this book.

Now is not the first time the future has veered in unpredictable directions, but it is the first time leaders have had "big data" and fast computers to analyze the changes. We must resist the temptation to assume that these analytical resources give us special powers to foretell the future when times are changing. All our existing data are measures of previous circumstances that are less and less likely to be repeated. Computers cannot compensate for data's historical limitations, and predictive models that use outdated data cannot tell us where we are going with an acceptable degree of certainty.

Trending toward Disorder

Things are not as they seem, nor are they otherwise.

Oriental wisdom

Sophisticated mathematical models could deal with this problem if we were headed from one steady state to another, but that is also unlikely in today's world. The current state of affairs suggests we are entering an era of prolonged instability instead: Our systems are trending toward disorder, rather than a new order, for the foreseeable future. Factors that controlled system dynamics in the past simply cannot be counted on to explain how things will work in the future. For example:

■ Not too long ago, decision makers could reasonably assume that the banking system provided a stable and reliable foundation for business in coming years. Collectively, financial institutions were rock solid. They could be counted on to manage money in expectable ways for customers' benefit (before "your money and our experience" became "our money and your experience"). Assets were secure. Prime rates had real meaning. Now, deregulated financial institutions are frequently engaged in speculative schemes with disastrous results; they are an element of uncertainty for decision makers. Banking can no longer be seen as a fundamental constant. If the banking system's future is unpredictable, predictions that assume financial stability may not be worth the paper they are printed on.

■ Governments were generally able to maintain economic and social equilibrium during the reign of predictive science in the last four decades of the twentieth century. Elected officials from different political factions could be counted on to compromise in the interests of moving things forward, slowly but surely, in expected directions. Gridlock now prevails, with no reliable assurances that things will return to normal any time soon. Diametrically opposed visions of the role of our government cast real doubt on the future. The situation around the world is just as unsettled. If governments cannot be counted on to provide predictable business conditions in the future, decision makers should not trust predictions extrapolated from relatively stable periods in the past.

■ Until recently, the population's demographic profile was not a significant independent variable in predictive models. Number of residents and rate of growth mattered, but predictions could be made without accounting for demographic details like age distribution and cultural diversity; shifts in these social metrics were gradual and had an inconsequential impact on system dynamics. We suddenly realize that an aging population—especially one that had expected secure retirement—and multicultural immigration are destabilizing in ways likely to make the future significantly different from the past. The future of our nation will trend in some unprecedented directions because its population is becoming very different. Predictions based on historical demographics are correspondingly misleading.

■ Not long ago, rules of the game were understood and enforced with acceptable consistency across our interacting systems. Public and private "watchdog" groups were expected to be honest and objective. Decision makers could plan for the future assuming that courts and regulatory agencies would continue to act consistently in the public interest. However, the last decade has shown that the referees cannot be trusted to enforce fair play in the future. Major players can flaunt convention with little fear of being penalized. We can no longer have total confidence in rating services, auditors, securities and insurance regulators, and many other enforcement agents.

■ Finally, the definition of reality itself seems to be undergoing radical transformation. We really do not know what is real anymore, making the future all the more uncertain for those who assume that fundamental concepts will be defined then as they are now. For example, a Supreme Court decision like *Citizens United v. Federal Election Commission* (a 2010 decision extending rights of free speech to corporations, thus allowing them to support or denounce candidates in elections) can create totally unpredictable shifts in the balance of political power and the business environment. Journalists are free to make up their own facts, with little or no fear of being held accountable in an era of "truthiness." Evidence of fraud in science is increasing at a disturbing pace.

Predictive modeling, then, must be replaced when it is based on assumptions that are no longer valid. The old tools no longer meet decision makers' needs because the rules of the game have changed and will not necessarily be enforced with reliable consistency. Therefore, we need to find new tools for figuring out where things are headed.

2. Violations of Model Assumptions

Even if predictive modeling were not nullified by discontinuities in system dynamics, the current practice of predicting almost always fails another acid test: Data from the system being modeled must comply with the predictive model's theoretical assumptions. For example, if a model is used to predict consumer response to an increase in the price of a prescription medication, it should use data describing what consumers actually paid—not the drug manufacturer's suggested retail price or the discounted price paid by insurance. The greater the discrepancy between a system's available data and the predictive model's assumptions about the data, the less believable the resulting predictions are.

Unfortunately, disturbingly large discrepancies between assumptions and data are common, and they are almost never mentioned, much less discussed, when predictions are made. Decision makers do not need to understand the finer details of this problem, but they do need to be sufficiently aware of it to raise questions about relevant predictions and to evaluate answers provided by the analysts who made them. This section provides just enough background information to help leaders avoid predictions derived from methods that violate critical assumptions. (Additional details can be found in resources listed at the end of the chapter.)

The theoretical importance of congruence between a predictive model's assumptions and a dynamic system's data is difficult to understand, but it does have real-world significance. How relevant is a model of demand for air travel that assumes all consumers are responding to the published full fare in coach? As we know, passengers on any flight pay a variety of prices and get different levels of service for their money. But, this assumptions-data link is almost never covered in basic college courses that introduce undergraduates to techniques of predictive modeling.

Only students in doctoral programs would be expected to understand the underlying mathematics well enough to identify and address relevant problems. Even specialists who understand the problem do not always take it seriously, which explains many bad predictions made over the past decade by PhD "quants" who should have known better. For example, big hedge fund losses have occurred when predicted supplies of agricultural crops did not reflect what farmers had actually planted or harvested.

Just as the general theory of predictive science requires consistent system dynamics over past and future time, the mathematical equations of predictive models also require consistent distribution of a key variable's data at a given point in time. The distribution is the array of individual values around a measure of central tendency for a common set of data. The classic illustration is the standard normal distribution, a bell-shaped curve with properties that provide the theoretical foundations for most inferential statistics: Its variations around the mean are perfectly symmetrical, and deviations are equal, above and below the mean.

Variation around the mean—the mean being the arithmetic average of all values—is expected in data from dynamic systems. For example, the Dow Jones Industrial Average is reported as a single number, but it is really a price-weighted statistical summary of the share values of 30 selected stocks, which have actual values above and below the spot average at any given point in time. This condition—an array of values around a representative measure of central tendency—exists for most key indicators from which predictions are made: interest rates, disposable incomes, consumer prices, unit sales, unemployed workers, agricultural yields, and so on.

Variations in Distribution Weaken a Model's Worth

Mathematical equations for making predictions from historical data are based on the assumption that the distribution of values has the same variation around the central measure over the relevant range, a condition known as homoscedasticity. The scatter plot on the left in Figure 3.1 illustrates a homoscedastic distribution. Deviations from the midpoint are uniform along the plot of data. Conversely, heteroscedasticity exists when variability is uneven across the range of the distribution. The heteroscedastic distribution in the scatter plot on the right shows uneven variation at different points along the range of values.

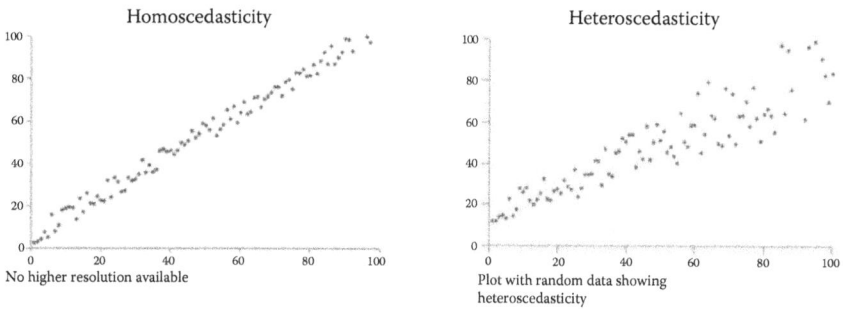

Homoscedasticity

No higher resolution available

Heteroscedasticity

Plot with random data showing heteroscedasticity

Figure 3.1 Homoscedastic and heteroscedastic distributions. (From Wikipedia.)

Linear regression equations can compute a historical "best-fit" trend line and extrapolate it into the future from both sets of data. However, interpretation of the resulting predictions should take into account the uneven variations in the respective distributions. A prediction derived from the heteroscedasticly distributed data would be less meaningful than one made from the homoscedastic data set, and the problem would become worse the more uneven the distribution. For example, dramatic redistribution of household income from the middle class to the top 5% bracket over the past decade casts doubt on predicted spending in many sectors of the economy (e.g., housing, durable goods, leisure activities).

The methodological problem is not variability of data per se. We could not make any predictions if real-world data had to be normally distributed because they almost never are; bell-shaped curves are the exception in databases that measure economic, business, social, and political activity. Rather, the problem is that predictive models embody critical assumptions about the independence of variables, and variations in the distributions of data for independent variables violate those assumptions. A model's suitability for calculating trends in historical relationships and extrapolating them into the future is correspondingly weakened.

━━━━━━━━━━━━━━━━━━━━━━━━━━━━━━━━━━━━

Special diagnostic tests (with interesting names like Koenker-Basset, Goldfield-Quandt, and Breusch-Pagan) have been developed to help analysts decide how big a grain of salt to use in interpreting predictions when data distributions are uneven. Unfortunately, the tests for evaluating compliance between a predictive model's assumptions and a dynamic system's data are almost never presented along with the predictions. Very few data analysts even bother to run the tests. In the rare instances when number crunchers conduct appropriate tests on a predictive model, diagnostic results are almost never reported because, surprise, the test results usually suggest the prediction should be interpreted with a lot of skepticism.

Statisticians and mathematicians who created the models and the tests would surely join me in concluding that resulting predictions are not to be trusted under such circumstances. From a methodological perspective, their models are better than the data. Unfortunately, good statisticians have no way to prevent an insensitive analyst from using their models to make meaningless predictions with uneven data.

This problem is unlikely to be resolved any time soon, if ever. Predictive models are built on critical assumptions that do not mesh with the uneven distribution of measurable characteristics of our highly diverse populations and multidimensional behaviors. Even if we assume that our data are accurate, the messy distribution of real-world numbers clashes with the ordered distribution assumptions of predictive models—one

"Frankly, Harold, you're beginning to bore everyone with your statistics."

more reason for decision makers to avoid predicting when
making plans for the future.

3. Deficiencies of Available Data

Even if system dynamics were reliably stable and if data consistently conformed to the requirement for symmetry, errors
in measurement and mistakes in transcription should make us
doubt many predictions. Models for extrapolating the past into
the future can be no better than the historical numbers that
are crunched, and predictions made from flawed data are likewise flawed. Unfortunately, we cannot automatically assume
that the numbers are accurate: The problem of meaningless or
error-ridden data is so widespread that no prediction should
be believed until the data behind it are verified.

In the not-too-distant past, people who used data were usually the same people who collected them. Conscientious researchers cared about the quality of measurement because they used their own numbers to study systems and make predictions. Collecting data also took a lot of time until computer networks started proliferating in the 1990s; before automated analytics, researchers often spent at least as much time collecting data as analyzing it—weeks, or even months. They knew they would be personally accountable for problems resulting from bad data because they usually had some responsibility for the entire process.

With few exceptions, researchers and analysts are now drowning in information collected without their direct involvement. They are seldom, if ever, invested in the measurements of the systems they study. This situation relieves them of personal responsibility for the quality of data they use to make predictions. To make matters worse, they can obtain lots of information to analyze at little or no cost—further relieving them of the need to decide if the numbers are worth anything. Pundits who argue information should be free need to be reminded that you get what you pay for.

Big Data

In the world of big data, computers now scan massive storage networks to assemble unprecedented amounts of information in almost no time at all. Consequently, students are currently taught how to search for data electronically, but they learn almost nothing about how to measure things accurately in the first place. We are almost never forced to ask questions about the quality of available numbers that measure economic and social systems; we take it for granted. "In data we trust" might be big data's unstated motto, but decision makers must remember that historical data do not point to the realm of future possibilities in unstable, dynamic systems. As shown in the following chapters and in the Postscript, big data are not a substitute for a crystal ball.

Ironically, the outstanding example of predictive science today—sabermetrics, better known as moneyball—is based on data that are the exception that proves the rule. Baseball statistics are remarkably good in comparison with the measures of most other activities. However, that does not mean predictive models used successfully in baseball are equally useful in other realms where the statistics are not as good. Business and government could rely more confidently on predictive science if they followed baseball's commitment to collecting meaningful numbers (and, of course, if they played a game where the rules changed very little over time and referees consistently enforced fair play).

Data users were constantly reminded to care about the quality of numbers well into the 1970s. Computer centers prominently displayed GIGO signs, for "garbage in, garbage out." (For younger readers, a computer center was a large room full of dumb terminals—somewhat like an Internet café— where users went for mainframe access before laptops and dial-up networks personalized computing in the 1980s. The terminals usually had to be reserved, and premium fees were charged for peak hour use. To save money, I did the computerized data analysis for my doctoral dissertation between midnight and 5 a.m.) Time on the computer was a scarce commodity; users were actively discouraged from running models with bad numbers because the results would be suspect, and someone else could have been using the computer.

Validity and Reliability

The two well-established measures of data quality are validity and reliability. Each of these concepts has specific, scientific definitions that should be used to evaluate the quality of data used for making predictions. Good predictions can only be made from valid and reliable data, assuming that all other conditions of predictive modeling have been met.

- *Validity* is a measure of the *meaningfulness* of data. It is the extent to which each variable used in a predictive model truly represents the phenomenon that is being projected into the future. For example, the unemployment rate is one of the most common variables used in predictions about future economic activity, but it is an invalid measure of the percentage of people in the labor force who would like to be working. The official definition of the labor force encompasses individuals who are working and those who are not working but looking for work. Unemployed people who give up hope of finding a job and quit looking ("discouraged workers") are no longer counted in the labor force, which causes the reported unemployment rate to fall. People who would like to be working but are not remove any meaning from the unemployment rate as a valid measure of the problem it presumably represents.
- *Reliability* is a measure of the *accuracy* of measurement. It requires that the precise values of variables in predictive models can be reproduced. Data are reliable to the extent that all values of a variable are measured on the same scale, one that is interpreted and recorded consistently by all individuals or devices involved in collecting the numbers. For example, data on prices are often unreliable, as illustrated, once again, by airline fares. On any given flight, passengers in the same cabin pay a wide range of

prices depending on when and where they bought the ticket, whether they had a discount coupon, how much extra they paid for baggage and amenities, whether they put the ticket on a credit card that added charges to the fare, and so on. Thus, historical ticket prices would be unreliable for predicting future costs of air travel.

Ironically, another problem with the reliability of data—intentional misrepresentation, or fraud, which we rarely consider—was illustrated as I boarded a flight at O'Hare shortly after starting to write this chapter. Talking into his cell phone, the passenger behind me said, "It's one of those cases where we are going to play with the data a bit. We'll slice and dice it as we need to." The person on the other end of the line was clearly being instructed to manipulate numbers as necessary to reach a conclusion not inferred by the original data.

Then, while reading on the long flight, I kept running into examples of deliberately bad data: articles in the *Wall Street Journal* and *New York Times* about a senior bank executive who admitted instructing analysts to change the dollar value of transactions—transactions that would be publicly reported to investors and regulators and used to predict market trends; articles in the same papers about intentional distortions in interbank loan and mortgage rates, which are frequently used to predict changes in various financial indexes; articles in *Science* and *Nature* magazines about falsification of research data in published studies that had been used to foretell major advances in medical treatments and later had to be retracted.

In short, leaders who base decisions on predictions should be attentive to the quality of the historical data used by the predictor. The more important the decision, the more carefully the decision maker should consider whether the data are meaningful and accurate—something not yet tested by intelligent software. Remember, good methodology cannot

*"These projected figures are a figment of our imagination.
We hope you like them."*

compensate for bad data (making GIGO an excellent choice of
screen saver for your digital desktop).

4. Failures of Previous Predictions

Thanks to a spate of recent books about the history of predicting, this section is mercifully short. Many prominent
authors have documented the endless flow of not-even-close
predictions in economic activity, market performance, political behavior, technological change, social transformation, and
so on. (See the list of resources at the end of this chapter.)
Certainly, journalists never have trouble finding examples
for their year-end stories comparing actual outcomes with

predictions made back in January; many of them take particular delight in comparing professional and random predictions, which inevitably show that dart throwers and coin tossers often do better than the professionals.

I honestly have nothing to add to the consensus: Predictions should be approached with considerable skepticism simply because they are so often wrong. I also note the absence of publications defending the opposite point of view. And, I remember a professor's quip from graduate school. He suggested the safest way to issue a prediction was to say what would happen but not when, or to say when a change would occur but not identify the change. Then, he delivered the punch line: If we had publicly stated what would happen *and* when it would happen *and* the prediction turned out to be correct, we should not act surprised.

In my field of expertise, medical economics, I cannot think of a single prediction about the impact of government health reforms since the passage of Medicare and Medicaid in 1965 that has ever been on the money. Experts always overestimate the savings to be produced by reform laws, usually by a very wide margin. One exception proves the rule: Predicted savings from Medicare Part D (adding drug coverage) were significantly underestimated—a nice surprise, but still a bad prediction. Any spending reductions that might ultimately be attributed to the Patient Protection and Affordable Care Act (ObamaCare) will almost certainly be swamped by higher costs of unintended consequences.

Although I am one of many commentators challenging the current practice of predicting because it is so often wrong, I am one of few—if not the only—to argue that predictive models should not even be used in many everyday applications. Others have offered well-reasoned proposals for refining methodology to improve the accuracy of models, but I do not believe better methods can or will meaningfully improve predictions in dynamically unstable systems.

Futurists who make bad predictions should consider the possibility that they are using the wrong tool for the job; the high prevalence of failed predictions is reason enough to look for a different one. Fortunately, as explained in the next chapter, a very different and appropriately aligned tool—forecasting—already exists for looking ahead in today's disordered operating environments.

5. Diversions from Strategic Innovation

Predicting poses one more serious problem when practiced outside the declining number of domains where we can reasonably expect the future to be an extension of the past: A prediction points to one expected outcome—a specific estimate of what will happen when—which then becomes the policy benchmark for business, government, and society at large. By encouraging us to push resources and direct activities to align with that single outcome, a prediction distracts decision makers from pursuing alternative futures that are not only possible but potentially preferable.

Predictive science draws on historical data that are, it is hoped, valid and reliable measures of what has already happened to estimate the values of decision variables for future states. This predetermined outcome is not a problem for anyone who is satisfied with historical trends—if the trends can be counted on to continue—and it is certainly consistent with the inherent inertia of systems lacking visionary leadership to take them in better directions. For better or worse, it leads to business as usual.

On the other hand, predictions cannot incorporate transformational changes that have not happened yet: future technologies, shifts in consumer preferences and spending power, rearrangement of relative prices, unprecedented laws and court decisions, geopolitical upheavals, demographic rearrangements, and so on. This limitation would not be a big deal if nothing big were changing, but the fact is that almost everything big is changing.

The very fact that the developed world is emerging so slowly from economic stagnation and political gridlock is probably due in some part to the enduring power of predictions. Governments and businesses tend to devote many resources to studying data and projecting them into the future in the process of making decisions. Assuming that leaders rely on the results to guide their actions, the common failure of predictions in the recent past could help explain the lack of progress over the past few years.

Predictions can even drain away hope that things will get better because the extrapolation of a problematic past logically leads to a problematic future, with a whole world of better alternatives ignored. Something important is missing here: Predictive science does not have any built-in mechanisms to enlarge our views of what is possible, let alone energize us to make big changes.

Creative Destruction

In *Capitalism, Socialism, and Democracy* (New York: Harper and Brothers, 1942), Joseph Schumpeter eloquently incorporated the problem of predictions in his theory of creative destruction—a concept enjoying a well-deserved renaissance because it links progress to replacing ways of doing things that have outlived their usefulness. The heroes of progress from the Schumpeterian perspective are people who could "think different" (e.g., Steve Jobs) and move people, products, markets, and governments onto a different path. None of the people who changed the world was motivated by a prediction because none of the changes they wrought was implied in historical data.

Visionary leaders are not the only sources of creative destruction. The world has been reshaped just as dramatically in the past few years by events that nobody could have foreseen purely by extrapolating data: The Arab Spring uprising, large-scale natural disasters, corporate failures due to fraud, massive immigration, and similar surprises that seem to be increasing in frequency as the world becomes more complex. Admittedly, we do not know if these disruptive events will ultimately lead to something new of value—a good operational definition of creativity—but they underscore the limitations of predictions.

There you are: five reasons why predictions ought to be abandoned in systems where the future will largely be determined by forces that did not determine the past. The good news is that there is a viable alternative, forecasting, that conforms much better to the new realities of our evolving world. Like predictive science, the science of forecasting is imperfect and evolving, but it embodies the assumption that the future is uncertain. Forecasting and its applications for decision makers are, happily, the subject of the rest of this book.

Additional Readings

Two recent books do an excellent job detailing the rampant problem of inaccurate predictions in a variety of recent applications. Honoring my pledge to avoid TMI (too much information), I refer you to Nate Silver's *The Signal and the Noise* (New York: Penguin Press, 2012) and Mark Buchanan's *Forecast: What Physics, Meteorology, and the Natural Sciences Can Teach Us about Economics* (New York: Bloomsbury, 2013).

For a focused overview of current applications in predictive modeling, see Siegel, Eric, *Predictive Analytics: The Power to Predict Who Will Click, Buy, Lie, or Die* (Hoboken, NJ: Wiley, 2013); and Mayer-Schonberger, Viktor, and Cukier, Kenneth, *Big Data: A Revolution that Will Transform How We Live, Work, and Think* (Boston: Houghton Mifflin, 2013).

Technical details about the theory and practice of predictive models are contained in Ratner, Bruce, *Statistical and Machine-Learning Data Mining: Techniques for Better Predictive Modeling and Analysis of Big Data,* 2nd edition (New York: CRC Press, 2011); and Wu, James, and Coggeshall, Stephen, *Foundations of Predictive Analytics* (New York: Chapman & Hall/CRC Data Mining and Knowledge Discovery Series, 2012).

Chapter 4

Forecasting

Introduction

To cross the conceptual bridge between predicting and forecasting, we cannot do better than consider the question of economic growth. Future changes in gross domestic product (GDP) are probably the paramount concern that private and public decision makers share. An army of analysts is constantly telling them what to expect, information that they use to set capital and operating budgets for the next fiscal period. Nearly all the analysts' predictions are derived from scientific models that use historical data, and the estimates vary widely. For example, initial predictions for 2012 GDP growth in the United States ranged from around +2% to +4%. Subsequent data suggest that the actual rate at year's end was approximately +2.2%, a figure near the bottom of the range. In other words, most of the predictions were wrong.

A forecast, in contrast, would estimate probabilities of possibilities that the 2012 GDP growth would deviate from the 2011 rate of +1.8%. My own forecast would have been a 20% chance that GDP growth would decline from the baseline (i.e., be less than +1.8%), a 50% chance that 2011's unimpressive rate would continue, and a 30% chance that the GDP would grow at a higher rate. I would have reviewed the predictive models while formulating my forecast, but I would also have carefully assessed the decision-making implications of qualitative forces not reflected in the models' historical data, including the economic status of our international trading partners and the impact of disastrous weather around the globe.

Such a forecast would have sensitized decision makers to a range of possibilities, and it would have been helpful. It also would have been unfamiliar because forecasts are seldom seen outside the realm of weather. Fortunately, professional weather observers have been learning how to anticipate a range of unpredictable events for more than a century, and their methodology—forecasting—provides a much better way to look into the crystal ball in today's chaotic world where many things are possible.

This chapter's discussion of the history and practice of weather forecasting sets the stage for a new tool for approaching the future of your own dynamic system, which is introduced in Chapter 5. (It also gives you a whole new appreciation for weather forecasts—you will be surprised how understanding changes in the weather can make you a better decision maker and manager. It has certainly helped me be a better health futurist.)

Forecasting's Foundations

Like predictive science before it, forecasting emerged as a branch of geophysics. Although forecasting has become the better method for speculating about futures in a wide variety of economic and political systems, its late nineteenth century origins grew almost exclusively from interest in the weather. Early land grant colleges collected and studied atmospheric information as part of their mission to improve crop and livestock production. The U.S. and Confederate armies reviewed weather data when making battle plans during the Civil War. Other federal agencies collected temperature and precipitation data as part of westward expansion, primarily so that geographers could define weather differences across the growing country at a particular point in time.

The government's information could not be used to estimate future weather at a particular point on the map until statistical tools became available in the late 1800s. Indeed, before the development of probabilistic quantitative analysis, the qualification for being a forecaster was living in an area long enough to have a sense of its normal weather patterns and being able to read seasonal skies based on experience. The development of descriptive statistics enabled a more scientific approach. The U.S. Weather Bureau was established in 1891 as a branch of the Department of Agriculture, and many clerks used the new statistical tools to tabulate weather data and study their patterns. Academic publications using their tables began to appear circa 1910.

Early atmospheric scientists theorized—correctly, but incompletely—that weather was explained by the simultaneous motion of water and heat, but they were not able to study the complex interactions of hydrodynamics and thermodynamics until computers were invented in the 1940s. The urgent need to incorporate weather into military planning during World War II suddenly directed many resources to development of scientific forecasting. The rapid expansion of commercial aviation created additional demand for weather reports at roughly the same time. A new job category, weatherman, was created. It was initially an art, not a science, and did not require a college degree.

Thanks to the invention of computers during the 1940s, scientific weather analysis evolved from obscure theory into widespread practice within just a few years. Not surprisingly, the pioneering work in atmospheric physics took place at the same universities and government facilities that developed the atomic bomb. Weather scientists, nuclear physicists, and rocket scientists competed for time on the few available computers to do their data analysis.

In her book on the history of modern meteorology, *Weather by the Numbers* (Cambridge, MA: MIT Press, 2012), Kristine Harper quoted a University of Chicago professor: "It is an unfortunate characteristic of meteorology that its great forward strides depend on disasters." Given that disasters and other unpredictable events are becoming more common, leaders in other kinds of dynamic systems should be motivated by weather forecasting's fast-track development in response to unpleasant circumstances. For example, meteorology's adaptation to adverse effects of global climate change should lead to better modeling techniques that can be used for forecasting in other dynamic systems.

From Predicting to Forecasting the Weather

In its early years, academic meteorology tried hard to become a predictive science. Weather was assumed to be just another natural phenomenon that could be explained mathematically, like planetary motion on the cosmic scale or chemical reactions at the molecular level. The military's desire for precise answers to critical questions (e.g., What will the weather be on Normandy's beaches at 5 a.m. on June 6, 1944?) caused early atmospheric scientists to focus on formulating, based on historical data, computer-solvable equations that could calculate future weather values for specific geographic locations. Their goal was dubbed numerical weather prediction (NWP). To develop the equations, researchers in government agencies and universities devoted considerable effort during the 1940s and 1950s to building weather simulation models.

The equations provided good representations of atmospheric phenomena, but the resulting weather predictions were unimpressive. They were wrong far more often than they were right, due in large part to the lack of computing power. Weather scientists never completely abandoned efforts to generate specific and accurate predictions—indeed, sophisticated NWP modeling is currently enjoying a renaissance to be addressed further in this chapter—but they were not able to satisfy people who needed to make decisions involving future weather events. Meteorology was forced to move in a practical direction that did not require extensive computational support.

Probabilities of different weather possibilities, rather than certainties of specific atmospheric conditions, seemed to be the best answer that weathermen could provide for questions about the future. Rather than predicting that 1.25 inches of rain would fall in Toledo the day after tomorrow, meteorologists started forecasting a 40% probability of rain there 2 days from now. Of course, a 40% chance of rain also means a 60% chance of something else. This "rest-of-the-story" component is seldom stated in a forecast, but it highlights forecasting's powerful focus on the big picture rather than a single outcome.

The Confidence Interval

Predicting's outlook is comparatively narrow in dynamic systems that can move in any number of directions. A prediction may seem to be acceptably accurate when stated with 95% confidence, but it does not draw attention to the other things that could happen. In fact, a 95% confidence interval is typically misunderstood to mean that the predicted outcome—such as the level of unemployment or the value of a stock market index 1 year from now—is 95% likely to occur (i.e., the possibility of all other outcomes is only 5%).

In reality, the confidence interval's mathematical complement, the level of statistical significance (p value), expresses nothing more than the probability that chance alone explains a predicted outcome. Confidence and statistical significance have nothing to do with the probability that the predicted event will actually happen, and they do not allude in any way to other possible outcomes. An absolute difference in a predicted outcome can be highly significant statistically—a difference explained by the model, not by random variation—but so small as to have no practical significance in the real world. (For example, after adjusting for random variation, the Food and Drug Administration [FDA] will usually approve a new drug if patients taking it live longer than patients not taking it, even though the difference might be as little as a few weeks.)

Once postwar weather researchers concluded that predictive modeling was too limited for evaluating future states of dynamic weather systems, they concentrated on developing the combined art and science of forecasting. The result, as illustrated by the huge conceptual difference between predicting 1.25 inches of rain and forecasting a 40% probability of precipitation, illustrates the core concept of forecasting. This is the reason why forecasting must replace predicting in any system where futures are unlikely to be defined solely by the past.

Most of us make decisions about our futures in dynamic environments that are much more like the fickle weather than the clockwork universe. Consequently, understanding how weather forecasts are made can be very instructive and pretty painless. As they say, it is not rocket science: It is what they do every day at the National Weather Service (NWS), not the National Aeronautics and Space Administration (NASA). Forecasting can be done just as beneficially in business, government, academia, and the nonprofit world by decision makers who want to prepare their organizations for better futures. Here is how the process works.

Identifying Explanatory Variables

Weather is a prototype of complexity. The deterministic, cumulative power of small events in large chaotic systems is usually illustrated with a global weather example—for example, the possibility that a tornado in Texas is initiated when a butterfly flaps its wings in Brazil. The first step toward understanding the butterfly effect's link between small, remote causes and big, local effects is identifying the variables that interact in a chain of causality from start to finish; what exactly happens, in what order, between the flapping of wings and the wind whipping up thousands of miles away?

In similar fashion, the general approach to forecasting starts by defining a system's causal variables and building a conceptual model from them. It then uses the model to evaluate the historical values of the variables, to interpret the quantitative results with informed judgment, and finally to assign probabilities to the possibilities. Again, it is art and science (which, in my experience, makes it much more fun than predicting, which is all science).

The factors that combine to create weather have been known for a long time. Aristotle recognized them nearly 2,500 years ago, defining *meteorology* as the study of things that fall out of the sky. Today, a common set of variables provides the foundation for most weather forecasting models. They are discussed here in the context of dynamic, interactive forces that forecasters must consider when assigning probabilities to the various weather possibilities.

The following overview of the general process of weather forecasting provides sufficient background knowledge for applying the power of forecasting to other domains, as explained in the next two chapters. This discussion of weather forecasting is simplified, but not simplistic, in remembrance of my promise not to provide TMI (too much information). (Several good meteorology books and classic articles are listed at the end of the chapter for readers who want a deeper understanding of how weather forecasters do their job.)

Most weather forecasting models include the following four causal variables, which combine in different ways to create a range of atmospheric conditions:

- Water: The chance of precipitation is usually the most important piece of information in a weather forecast because people make important decisions based on the prospects for rain, hail, sleet, or snow. These basic weather events are made possible by the amount of atmospheric water available to shift from its gaseous phase (water vapor) to a liquid or solid state (water or ice). Hydrodynamics is arguably what makes weather so interesting to us.
- Temperature: From the forecast user's point of view, knowing whether the weather will be warm or cold is almost as important as knowing whether it will be wet or dry. That is because water's ultimate manifestation as weather is a direct function of the temperature of the air in which it is suspended: If the temperature goes below zero, the water turns into a solid and falls to the earth as snow or ice. Temperatures above freezing but below boiling have proportional effects on the formation and type of clouds and rainfall. Surface heating, impacted by snow on the ground or clouds in the sky, is another key consideration.

■ Pressure: The weight of an air mass above the earth's
surface creates atmospheric pressure: the heavier the air,
the greater the pressure. The movement of water and
temperature is directly linked to pressure, so evaluation
of pressure gradients helps identify where weather events
are likely to occur. (Atmospheric pressure's importance
as a forecasting variable is well known to people whose
joints or moods flare up just before the weather changes.)
Pressure differences often make the edges of weather
systems quite visible to the naked eye—specific types of
cloud formations are associated with frontal boundaries
and the types of weather that are likely to follow.

■ Wind: Direction and speed of wind flow are likewise
fundamental considerations. They indicate where a column of air (called a *parcel*) is potentially headed and
how quickly it might get there. Atmospheric wind has
two important components—horizontal and vertical—that
determine how moist air will be transformed into weather
by variations in temperature and pressure at and above
a geographic location. The interplay of horizontal and
vertical flow is a particularly important determinant of the
severity of weather—a major factor for public safety officials who must decide if people should evacuate an area
threatened by a major storm.

A good forecaster needs to understand not only the importance of each variable, but also all their possible interactions.
For example, the weather potential of a fixed amount of mois-
ture in the air varies substantially with the temperature of the
air: The weather could be sunny and dry during the day, with
fog forming overnight as the same air mass cools. Given the
wide range of possible values for each individual variable and
the number of possible interactions between and among them,
weather forecasters must deal with remarkable complexity.
Models simplify their work and make it manageable.

"And in the Dakotas—plenty of this!"

Specifying the Model

Specification is the art of choosing causal variables to include in a model. It is an art because forecasters use different variables, reflecting their personal experiences and interpretations of atmospheric phenomena—for example, some forecasters specialize in forecasting snow, others in hazardous summer storms. Model specification is the most fundamentally human step in making a forecast because it requires careful a priori thought about the system in question. Like painters and composers, individual forecasters even modify their models over time in response to lessons learned from previous efforts and ongoing changes in the environment.

The four-variable model we just considered is a common one, used by many television and radio forecasters to look at the weather for a local area for a media outlet with limited resources. Organizations responsible for national forecasts tend to have larger budgets that allow them to develop conceptual models with more variables (i.e., to spend more money on data collection and computing power). However, as you will see in the following, bigger is not necessarily better.

If model specification were a pure science, like calculating the trajectory of a rocket or the heat generated by a chemical reaction, all forecasters would use the same model based on the same proven laws and obtain the same results. Replicability, as we have seen, is a basic scientific principle. Computers can easily scan data and fit a mathematical equation to a pattern in the numbers, but their software lacks the experience and insight to differentiate between random patterns and meaningful relationships. A model with a strong mathematical fit can be completely meaningless in the real world when the underlying relationship is the result of chance—always a possibility. This problem is much more serious than many predictive analysts would like to admit.

The forecaster's first step in model specification is to envision plausible dynamic relationships within a system. Statistical tools can test data for violations of the model's assumptions after it has been specified, but thinking must come first. Familiarity with the modeled system is therefore very important for a forecaster. The best weather forecasters have usually spent years observing local weather and fine-tuning their models based on experience over time. Good forecasters also know that an area's weather patterns do not evolve with mathematical precision. Because unprecedented forces can change a system's dynamics, a good forecaster is always thinking about substituting a new variable for an old one, such as substituting airborne particulates for cloud cover if air pollution becomes a significant determinant of local weather. (Remember that *unfinished* is one of the key words in the definition of a model in Chapter 2.)

The second essential step in specifying a model—one not always taken—is selecting a limited number of independent, causal variables that contribute collectively to changes in the dependent variable. Statistical tools can help eliminate redundant or conflicting variables, but they cannot compensate for the limitations of human capacity to understand dynamic systems or of mathematics to represent real-world complexity. The clear consensus is that a good model has no more than four or five variables. The best forecasters tend to focus on learning more about the variables already in their models than on finding others to add.

Including too many variables in a model, a problem called overspecification or specification error, is common in forecasting (and in predicting, for the same methodological reasons). A model with more than four or five variables might seem to be more complete than one with fewer, but it can actually have less explanatory power. That is because the addition of too many variables violates statistical assumptions concerning independence and error correlation. Adding variables has the effect of explaining more and more about less and less until absolutely everything is explained about nothing.

If one variable contributes relatively little to the forecast, good methodological practice suggests replacing it with a different variable that has more explanatory power; in the same way, if changes in a system's dynamics suggest adding a new variable, the appropriate response is to usually delete one at the same time. Again, a priori thought should guide the substitution: Allowing a computer to find the "best" replacement variable by comparing all possible combinations of variables (known as stepwise substitution) runs the serious risk of discovering—and relying on—a random pattern in the data.

The fundamental importance of simplicity in modeling has been recognized for nearly a millennium. William of Ockham (1285–1349) issued a famous challenge that has been endorsed and practiced by virtually every famous philosopher, scientist, and engineer since then: "Never increase, beyond what is necessary, the number of entities required to explain everything." Today's less-elegant version of Ockham's razor is "keep it simple, stupid" or KISS. However it is expressed, meteorology shows simplicity is the better approach to forecasting—an important lesson for decision makers who apply forecasting in other dynamic systems.

Measuring the Explanatory Variables

Serious problems with validity and reliability of data have already been identified as one of the reasons why predictions are so often wrong. Weather forecasting is no less vulnerable to bad numbers, so modeling's success depends on the quality of measuring, reporting, storing, and retrieving relevant data. Decision makers who shift from predicting to forecasting in other dynamic systems need to be sure their crystal balls (i.e., conceptual models) are primed with meaningful, accurate numbers.

Improvements in the accuracy of weather forecasts are due in no small measure to improvements in the quality of meteorological data. The number and geographic dispersion of ground weather stations have grown substantially from a handful of unevenly distributed airports over the past few decades, making it possible for meteorologists to issue forecasts for smaller local areas. In addition, atmospheric scientists tend to pay close attention to the precise definition of variables and consistent calibration of data-gathering instruments. (In my experience, today's weather information is generally much more accurate and complete than information about the economy and health care. Many major failures of economic policy and health reform can be attributed to bad data.)

Real-time atmospheric information from airplanes and satellites also improves the accuracy of forecasts. Indeed, availability of three-dimensional data is one of the biggest advances in atmospheric science in the past 50 years. When I was doing hailstorm research back in the 1960s, vertical observations came from a single weather balloon launched early each morning; readings from devices measuring wind speed and direction were usually outdated by the time storms formed in the afternoon. Today's ground and air data tend to be available to forecasters within minutes of collection; satellite photos of cloud formations and wind patterns are equally current and enormously helpful, as are reports from airplane pilots.

Ongoing improvement in forecasts, then, is arguably due more to improvements in information—increases in the quantity of basic weather data, improvements in the graphics used to display it, and increases in the speed with which it can be analyzed—than to improvements in meteorological theory. Consequently, one of meteorology's lessons for forecasters in other dynamic systems is the need to pay careful attention to the quality of the numbers they analyze. Weather forecasting is not a perfect science, but its practitioners have done a much better job than their counterparts in many other applications of predictive science because meteorologists tend to focus on good data rather than more data. Forecasting's emphasis on quality over quantity is particularly noteworthy at a time when the next big thing is big data for predictive analytics.

Analyzing Variations over Time

If weather were predictable, weather forecasters would simply extrapolate the factors that caused today's weather to tomorrow—a practice known as *persistence forecasting* in the uncommon situations when air masses are stuck in one place (i.e., stable) from one forecast period to the next. This approach makes no sense when the atmosphere is in its normally dynamic state. The variables that caused today's weather in a given area almost always dissipate or move to another location, where they explain tomorrow's weather someplace else.

The classic approach to anticipating weather for a specific area is called *analog forecasting*. It is based on the appropriately simple concept (remember Ockham's razor) that constant changes in local weather follow consistent patterns over the long run, but not from day to day. Interaction of the weather variables at any given point in time is assumed to be unpredictable due to the incredible complexity of atmospheric events (remember the butterfly effect), but the realm of possibilities is generally defined for a given forecast area. For example, the typical weather in Chicago is well known, but it is different from typical weather in Seattle, Denver, Dallas, Atlanta, or Boston.

People traveling between any two of these cities would reasonably expect the weather to be different on arrival in the other; however, they would not know exactly what to expect due to hour-to-hour and day-to-day variations in each city's characteristic weather patterns. Analog forecasting is the basic approach that weather experts have used for more than a century to help visitors and locals decide how to prepare for their planned activities—what to wear, whether to take an umbrella, how much extra time to allow for travel, when to plant the garden, and so on. As its name implies, the analog approach to forecasting answers the questions by estimating probabilities of different possibilities from analogous sequences in historical weather data for a forecast area.

The analog forecaster's tasks, in rough order, are to:

■ determine current values of the weather variables
■ scan historical data and identify times when previous values were identical to current values

- determine subsequent weather events on the following days in history
- compute the relative frequencies (i.e., probabilities) of the different events

Assume that today's 6 a.m. weather values are relative humidity of 45%, temperature of 55°F, barometric pressure of 30.21 inches, and winds out of the southwest at 15 miles per hour. So, we search the historical weather data to find the previous 100 days when the values were comparable at 6 a.m. Then, to prepare a midday forecast, we identify the midday weather for each of the 100 similar days. (Computers now do this in an instant.)

If rain showers occurred 6 hours later on 30 of the previous 100 days that started out just like today, the forecast would be a 30% chance of rain showers around noon today—all other things being equal. Of course, the data search would also identify the other 70% of possibilities, such as a 40% chance of clear skies, a 10% chance of a severe thunderstorm, and so on. (As already noted, these other percentages are almost never reported today.) The analog forecasting process can also be extended to see what happened at other historic time intervals, such as 1 and 2 days later. However, reliability drops off quickly, and analog forecasts are seldom made beyond 5 days.

Assembling the Forecast

The practical value of classical analog forecasting is enhanced by regular discussions among forecasters who use different models, work in geographically adjacent forecast areas, or have special expertise in relevant factors like the jet stream or large-scale weather systems. This interactive process, known as *consensus forecasting*, is both productive and interesting.

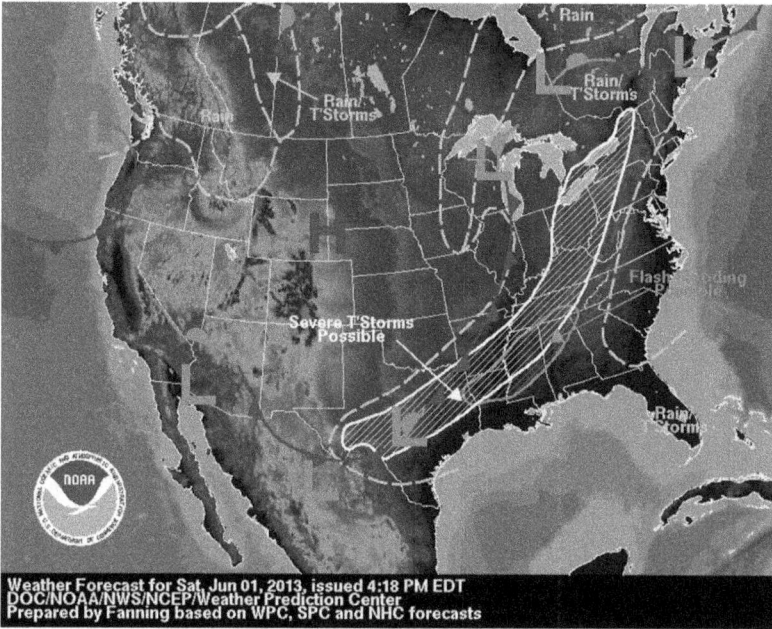

Weather Forecast for Sat, Jun 01, 2013, issued 4:18 PM EDT
DOC/NOAA/NWS/NCEP/Weather Prediction Center
Prepared by Fanning based on WPC, SPC and NHC forecasts

Figure 4.1   National weather forecast map. (From National Oceanographic and Atmospheric Administration, http://www.nws. noaa.gov/outlook_tab.php.)

(Actual discussions can be followed for each local forecast area in the NWS's Area Forecast Discussions at www.noaa.gov). Conversations among meteorologists provide an excellent forum for learning about forecasting in general. Warning: Reading the NWS's consensus discussions may turn you into a weather addict.)

Before issuing final forecasts based on their own models and consensus discussions, most meteorologists visually review weather maps known as synoptic charts, which summarize weather variables nationally (see Figure 4.1) and from surrounding forecast areas (see Figure 4.2). This common practice emphasizes the art of forecasting and the importance of studying how water, temperature, pressure, and wind move across the land and create weather. It also casts severe doubt

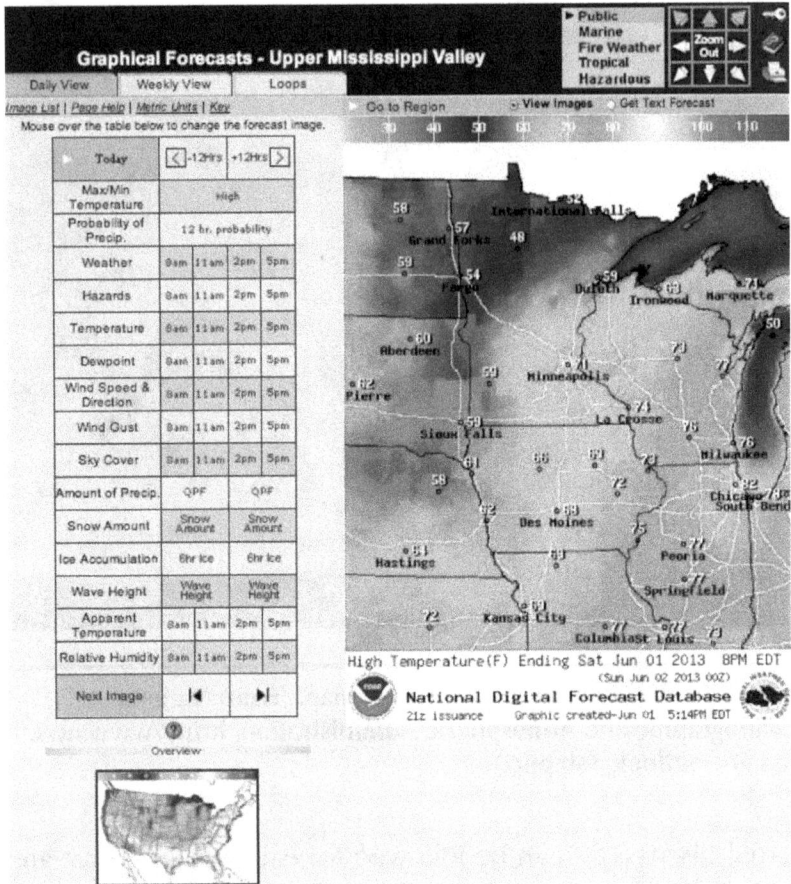

Figure 4.2 Regional synoptic weather forecast map. (From National Oceanographic and Atmospheric Administration, http://graphical. weather.gov/sectors/uppermissvly.php?element=MaxT.)

on one-size-fits-all approaches to forecasting and provides an important foundation for the discussion in Chapter 5 of how to forecast in other dynamic systems.

Of course, many atmospheric physicists have continued to pursue strictly numerical techniques for projecting future weather. The ongoing debate between proponents of classical forecasting and computer-generated predicting—a friendly and professional dialogue, as near as I can tell—has produced two hybrid approaches that are now used in varying degrees by most meteorologists. The concepts behind these refinements can also be applied to forecasting the future of other dynamic systems.

Ensemble forecasting was developed in the 1990s to address persistent problems with the accuracy of fully automated projections of chaotic systems. It is fundamentally a predictive method, but it uses a well-accepted statistical technique (Monte Carlo analysis) to derive a sample of predictions from different initial conditions. By producing multiple simulations from a single set of meteorological data, it generates a distribution of possible outcomes and corresponding probabilities defined by the distribution. In effect, ensemble forecasting synthesizes a forecast from many predictions and embodies random variation in the process. Although ensemble forecasts have not proven to be demonstrably better than other models for estimating future weather, they have definitely proven to be better than single predictions. Even traditional forecasters now regularly review "ensembles" to inform their subjective analysis of weather trends.

Ingredients-based forecasting is the other major variation on numerical weather predicting that was developed in response to limitations of fully computerized approaches. Here, the recipe analogy works: The process begins with careful analysis of an existing, well-documented weather event—just as chefs might examine a finished entrée that they have never seen before—and then works backward to identify the key ingredients, their quantities, and the processes that produced the final outcome. In effect, a high-powered computer analysis of extensive data about, say, a thunderstorm emulates the subjective analysis of a meteorologist, who has dedicated an entire career to studying the same event. Once the recipe for a specific storm has been retrospectively created, it tells the weather forecaster what is likely to happen the next time the same ingredients converge under the same conditions. It can be filed in a meteorological "cookbook" and retrieved through a search of key ingredients.

Model Guidance for Sandy–4 days before landfall

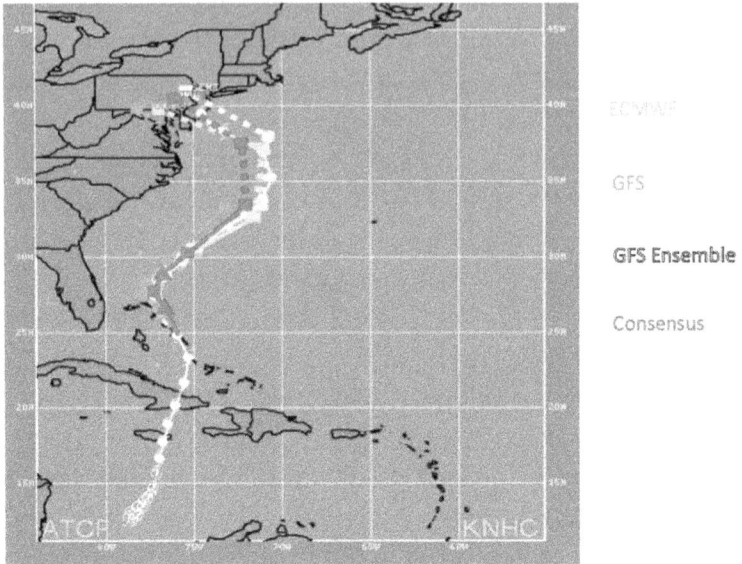

Figure 4.3 Center points of four forecast models for Hurricane Sandy, 4 days before landfall. (From National Hurricane Center Outreach Resources, http://www.nhc.noaa.gov/outreach/.)

Several different weather forecasting models are in daily, simultaneous use simply because the earth's atmosphere is a chaotic system. Figure 4.3 demonstrates this point visually, showing the variations in four different models' projected point of landfall 4 days before Hurricane Sandy hit the East Coast on October 29, 2012. The underlying complexity is greater than the representational capabilities of any single model. (It is the old specification problem: Models become meaningless when they include too many variables.) Meteorologists in each model's camp are continually trying to improve the accuracy of their approach while learning what they can from the others. None can realistically expect to develop a model that will vanquish the others because weather and climate are constantly changing in unpredictable ways—unlike clockwork universes that can be projected into the future with mathematical precision.

Meteorology offers two lessons for decision makers who want to forecast the future in other dynamic systems, such as transportation or banking:

- Constantly seek to improve your perceptual knowledge of the causal variables and the changing climate, and
- Don't expect a computer to give you all the answers.

Forecasting's enduring value is reinforced by its survival in a discipline in which many researchers have assiduously pursued the theoretical precision of predicting. The evolution of weather forecasting since World War II suggests that art and science together will generally produce the most accurate image in a crystal ball.

Interpreting a Forecast

Assuming it does not fall into methodological traps detailed in the previous chapter, a prediction has appeal because it is objective. It nevertheless has a good chance of being wrong in a complex, dynamic system in which many outcomes are possible. Deciding whether a prediction was right or wrong is easy in the final analysis because the predicted value either did or did not occur at the appointed time.

In comparison, the process for judging a forecast's accuracy is subjective—a lesson I learned long ago when forecasting hailstorms and other severe weather in northeastern Colorado. After all, statisticians have never agreed on a uniform definition of probability. (That is a story I will not tell here, in honor of the pledge for not providing TMI.) To illustrate the fundamental problem, let us assume I had forecasted a 50% probability of a thunderstorm with hail tomorrow. If no hail occurred anywhere in the forecast area on the following day, my forecast was just as correct as if hail had fallen.

A forecaster's real success can only be judged over time. If I issued 10 next-day forecasts with a 50% chance of hail-producing thunderstorms and hail fell somewhere in the forecast area on 5 of the following days, I was correct 100% of the time. However, for the same reason that 10 consecutive flips of a coin occasionally produce 10 heads or 10 tails, if hail did not fall at all during that time, I am not necessarily a dismal failure as a forecaster. This eventuality, like the all-heads or all-tails outcome, is very uncommon, but it can happen when outcomes are determined by a random—that is, unpredictable—event. A string of bad forecasts can just be bad luck. (Of course, I must admit that 100% success could also be due to good luck.) Judging a forecaster requires a lot of forecasts, for the same reason that meaningful statistical analysis requires a lot of samples.

There is another way to look at the problem of defining a forecast's accuracy. Assume that my forecast area is 100 miles by 100 miles square, a fairly typical situation. A 50% forecast of a thunderstorm is 100% accurate if tomorrow's hailstorm only passes over half the area, even though people in the dry area will probably judge it badly. Judging forecasts over space (i.e., geographically) is much less common than judging them over time, but it is a legitimate approach.

The accuracy of weather forecasts is a decreasing function of time and space, even for the best forecasters. Short-term forecasts are consistently more accurate than long-term forecasts, and small-area forecasts are better than large-area forecasts. It is the butterfly effect again; prospects for feedback-driven chaos increase the greater the distance or the longer the time from a causal event. This is important for decision makers who want to anticipate futures in their own dynamic system: They need to assess the limits of how far ahead they can meaningfully look. Making the switch from predicting to forecasting creates awareness of possibilities, but it does nothing to overcome instabilities that grow over time and space.

To understand the practical significance of this point, remember that my hypothetical 50% forecast of a hail-producing thunderstorm was correct because half the area experienced a severe storm, and the other half did not. Decision makers approaching the future with a 50% forecast, such as farmers wondering whether to plant or airlines wondering whether to reroute flights, will want to prepare for several possibilities in different areas. On the other hand, many decision makers who respond to a numeric weather prediction for their area (e.g., between zero and several inches of rain) are going to be unexpectedly dry or wet.

What Makes a Good Forecaster?

If your head is whirling at this point, it is understandable. Trying to figure out the future of manufacturing or the travel industry will be just as mind boggling, given the scarcity of certainty in complex systems. Just remember, the trick to interpreting a forecast is not to figure out which of the possibilities is correct; rather, it is to plan for the possibility that several different outcomes can—and quite likely will—occur simultaneously. Good forecasters sensitize people to the realm of possibilities and alert them to opportunities to prepare.

Weather forecasters regularly confront a related issue that will need to be addressed as forecasting is adopted in other dynamic systems: They can use their best verbal and visual skills to explain forecasts, but people in the audience do not always understand the message. For example, recent forecasts of hurricanes along the East Coast have been remarkably accurate, but for a variety of reasons, many residents in affected areas have not taken them seriously. Forecasters are now working with social scientists and communications specialists to improve their abilities to communicate meaningfully with a very diverse audience; a single forecast may need to be stated in several different ways to have its desired impact on different segments of the affected population. There is much work to be done to optimize the impact of good forecasts in *any* system, including business and government.

Finally, an important hallmark of a good forecaster is personal detachment; biased forecasts are every bit as dangerous as biased predictions. A weatherman or -woman who wants to play golf over the next few days might be tempted to forecast clear skies, but this is "wishcasting"—if not fraudulent forecasting—when the weather variables suggest a storm is likely. Conversely, public pressure can be a factor; forecasters in drought-ridden areas have been known to report that listeners in their audience want a forecast of rain, as if it might create a self-fulfilling prophecy.

As a decision maker, you should seek forecasters whose track records show they are willing to consider and assess all possibilities with an open mind, suppressing personal preferences or audience desires. Forecasters should demand equal objectivity from analysts whose predictions will be factors in the process of forecasting. (For what it is worth, my current forecasts for the future of American health care are quite inconsistent with my personal political views and my ideal design for the medical economy.)

Incorporating the Role of Climate Change

Atmospheric science is built on a powerful concept: climate. In meteorology, climate is the set of fixed factors that shape interaction of the weather variables—in its simplest form, the collection of physical characteristics covered in an introductory geography class.

- *Terrain*: One of the most basic dimensions of climate is the difference between water and land. Water's influence on weather depends on its breadth and depth: The interaction of weather variables is different over the ocean than over an inland lake, but both bodies of water help shape the surrounding weather. Land has a wider range of climatic characteristics, from rocks to soil, fields to forests, pavement to lawns, and so on. In addition, a given land parcel's impact on weather is affected by surface cover and cloud cover, which create feedback loops and make outcomes literally unpredictable.
- *Altitude*: Weather varies significantly with absolute differences in height above sea level. For example, Mexico City and Los Angeles have similar terrains, but they have different weather patterns due to the 7,000-foot difference in their altitudes. Relative differences in the altitude of local terrains also matter: Two cities at the same altitude will usually have different weather patterns if one is surrounded by foothills and the other is in the middle of an extended plain.
- *Latitude*: Areas with the same terrain and altitude will have different weather depending on their distances from the equator. Forecasting models for tropical, middle-latitude, and polar areas are different because geophysical forces vary significantly with the velocity of the earth's rotation, the angle of the earth's orbit, and exposure to the sun.

Climate factors are fixed. They do not vary during a forecast period, so they cannot be variables in forecasting models for local areas. However, identical values of weather variables will tend to produce different weather in different climates. The parameters previously used as the 6 a.m. baseline for assembling a forecast (relative humidity of 45%, temperature of 55°F, barometric pressure of 30.21 inches, and winds out of the southwest at 15 miles per hour) will play out differently in Denver and Dallas on the same day due solely to differences in climate. The day-to-day weather in both cities will vary unpredictably within the limits determined by local climate, but the variations will not be the same.

Meteorologists have a saying that nicely summarizes the point: Climate is what you expect; weather is what you get. This explicit recognition of climate's role in explaining variations in weather is one more reason why leaders in other dynamic systems should use forecasting to shape their approach to the future—forecasting is sensitive to differences in climate; predicting is not. Consequently, the most important reason for forecasting the future in any dynamic system relates to the same realization that is revolutionizing meteorology—climates change.

Climate change is so powerful and so pervasive in today's world that it compels us to expand our perception of the realm of possibilities. We all know that local weather is not what it used to be:

- Storms of the century are occurring every few years now.
- Rising ocean levels are threatening coastal communities all around the world, not just Venice and Amsterdam.
- Hurricanes are bigger than ever.
- Entire regions known for their abundant crops are suddenly experiencing droughts of unprecedented duration.
- Some century-old winter festivals have not been held for several years now due to lack of ice and snow.

Atmospheric and geophysical scientists believe almost without exception that these new weather patterns are produced by global climate change (something different from global warming). A large and growing body of published research findings supports their consensus. Altitude and latitude have not changed anywhere in the world over the past century, but terrain sure has. The replacement of vegetation with concrete (e.g., urbanization, deforestation) and the generation of heat from combustion are more than enough to explain unprecedented changes in the weather all around the world.

I personally experienced the power and rapidity of climatic change when studying violent storms in Colorado's eastern plains. Denver, long known as the queen city of the plains, had never had a tornado when our research project commenced in the early 1960s; cool air flowed eastward over the mountains in summer afternoons, but it had to move at least 30 miles beyond Denver to mix with enough hot air to create a tornado. At the same time, the city boomed economically: The metropolitan population nearly doubled between 1960 and 1970.

Denver was suddenly filled with radiating heat sinks—skyscrapers, highways, and parking lots to accommodate all the workers who drove heat-generating cars in from the suburbs. Air pollution reached dangerous levels by the mid-1960s (Denver's infamous "brown cloud"). The city's first tornado occurred in 1967, and twisters quickly became common there. A meteorologist at the University of Chicago studied the change in Denver's climate and discovered that the atmospheric energy generated by growth could easily account for the sudden, unprecedented appearance of tornadoes.

Given the unprecedented changes taking place in virtually every aspect of our daily lives, leaders in public and private positions will make much better decisions about the future when they understand and apply the concept of climate change in their own dynamic systems. As the saying goes, think globally and act locally. We are all buffeted by external changes that are largely beyond our control, but we must take them into account as we look in our individual crystal balls.

Expecting the Unexpected

When I shifted employment from the National Center for Atmospheric Research in Boulder to Penrose Hospital in Colorado Springs in 1969, my new colleagues in health care were fascinated by my prior experience with weather forecasting. The hospital's chief executive officer (CEO), Sister Myra James Bradley, even had me give a seminar on the topic. At the end of my presentation, she made a wonderful observation that provides an appropriate conclusion for this chapter. Referring to the sudden addition of tornadoes to Denver's realm of weather possibilities, I spoke about the need to assign a probability to unprecedented and unforeseeable outcomes. She instantly dubbed it the "God only knows" (GOK) factor.

The possibility of GOK should be considered for inclusion in every forecast. Any dynamic system can now experience outcomes for which there is absolutely no precedent. Complexity is growing rapidly *and unpredictably* in almost every aspect of our daily lives. Unprecedented events are generally not pleasant to imagine—nightmares like the "big one" (earthquake) on the West Coast, a solar flare that wipes out communications, or a new form of terrorism—but they cannot be ignored.

The GOK in our futures is similar to the "black swan" phenomenon appropriately popularized by Nicholas Nassim Taleb in his best-selling book, *The Black Swan: The Impact of the Highly Improbable* (New York: Random House, 2007). However, GOK is even more powerful because it forces us to think about things that do not yet exist, that have not yet happened. Black swans already exist; we just do not see them very often.

Predictions do not allow for GOK outcomes: Something that has never happened simply will not be foretold in a predictive model. A new weather phenomenon will not be revealed in a mechanical, numbers-only weather forecast. Thankfully, modern meteorology recognizes the value of experienced, objective human involvement in processes for looking at the future. Weather forecasters are drawing on art and science to enhance their ability to view future possibilities; the forecasting models described in this chapter provide useful tools for anticipating turbulent times in just about every system in which the rest of us operate. Thank you, meteorology, for providing the insights to upgrade our crystal balls.

Forecasting's relevance to today's unpredictable world takes us back to another future-focused process that took hold in the 1960s: strategic planning. Peter Drucker and a few other business visionaries developed this powerful business tool that deserves a renaissance. Therefore, the rest of this book is a practical how-to guide for generating forecasts (Chapter 5) and synthesizing them with strategic planning (Chapter 6) to create better futures in any kind of dynamic system. This is the core concept of upgrading the crystal ball: developing new ideas of where we could be, far from our old paths when desirable, and developing plans for getting us there.

Additional Readings

Extensive information about the historical development of weather forecasting is presented in Harper, Kristine C., *Weather by the Numbers: The Genesis of Modern Meteorology* (Cambridge, MA: MIT Press, 2012); and Roulstone, Ian, and Norbury, John, *Invisible in the Storm: The Role of Mathematics in Understanding the Weather* (Princeton, NJ: Princeton University Press, 2013). Both books describe the history of meteorology in other countries and important international collaborations. An overview of key issues is presented in Doswell, Charles A., "The Human Element in Weather Forecasting," *National Weather Digest* 11(2):6–18, 1986.

Readers who are interested in becoming advanced amateurs at weather forecasting will find useful material in Dunlop, Storm, *Firefly Guide to Weather Forecasting* (Buffalo, NY: Firefly Books, 2010); and Keen, Richard A., *Skywatch West: The Complete Weather Guide*, revised edition (Golden, CO: Fulcrum, 2004). A good, basic textbook used in academic meteorology programs is Lackman, Gary, *Midlatitude Synoptic Meteorology: Dynamics, Analysis, and Forecasting* (Boston: American Meteorological Society, 2011).

Classic articles on specific forecasting models include Wetzel, Suzanne W., and Martin, Jonathan E., "An Operational Ingredients-Based Methodology for Forecasting Midlatitude Winter Season Precipitation," *Weather Forecasting* 16:156–167, 2001); and Stensrud, David J., Brooks, Harold E., Du, Jun, Tracton, Steven, and Rogers, Eric, "Using Ensembles for Short-Range Forecasting," *Monthly Weather Review* 27:433–446, 1999.

Chapter 5

Forecasting in Dynamic Systems

Surely we will end up where we are headed if we do not change direction.

—Confucius

Unless you are a meteorologist, you should be wondering by now how to forecast the future of your own dynamic system—be it technology, manufacturing, media, logistics, retail, professional services, hospitality, banking, social services, government, or some other sector. (I assume that anyone who thinks predicting meets all their needs has already quit reading this book.) The previous chapter explained the classic forecasting model, but you will need to tailor it to the particular climate of your industry.

This chapter provides practical guidelines to get you started, based on the well-established methods from meteorology that I have applied as a health futurist for the past 40 years. However, this is not a cookbook. A universal approach to forecasting would not make sense because every sector of the economy has its own history, its own unique realm of possibilities, and its own set of accelerating changes. I can walk you through the science, but you will have to supply your own creativity on the artistic end of forecasting.

As we have seen, the four or five best variables in a forecasting model will not be the same in every system, and occasional substitutions will need to be made over time to adjust for climate change. A model is "imperfect, oversimplified, and *unfinished*," so you can expect to be fine-tuning for as long as the future matters.

I perform a careful evaluation of my health industry forecasting model every January, or more frequently if I perceive a significant midyear change in climate or other environmental factors (e.g., a game-changing Supreme Court decision, discovery of a cure for a major disease, government failure to implement a key provision of a reform law). This annual review tends to result in replacing one variable with another approximately every other year; starting with a five-variable model, I replace rather than add to avoid weakening the model with too many variables. Forecasting models may need to be changed more or less often in other systems. The key is to create a regular, systematic process for looking at the future in yours without creating specification error.

Ready? Here we go.

How to Identify Explanatory Variables

The first step in model building is choosing the explanatory variables that, together, will provide a good picture of the dynamics in your public or private sphere. As you might guess, people who make predictions are interested only in variables that can be expressed as numbers, manipulated mathematically, and analyzed statistically, so they generally go to existing data resources to find the variables and values for their models. In economic forecasting, these are typically derived from data published by government agencies (e.g., the Department of Commerce's Bureau of Labor Statistics, Department of Agriculture's Economic Research Service, Department of the Treasury's Financial Data Directory).

But, we know that numbers cannot describe or explain everything that happens in a dynamic system. Even the clock-work universe is not quantified at its smallest and largest dimensions; particle physicists and cosmologists still do not know what to look for, much less measure, at the extremes. That is why you, as a forecaster, will undoubtedly find one or more nonquantifiable forces important enough to be among your model's variables. In retail, for example, one might be a composite measure of consumers' style or brand preferences; in automobile insurance, it might be perceptions of online customer services.

My general advocacy of forecasting over predicting in dynamic systems must not be interpreted as outright rejection of objective measurement in favor of subjective assessment. Both forms of observation are critical to any process of examining future possibilities, as long as the observations are valid and reliable, so you should be prepared to select a mix of qualitative and quantitative variables that currently explain your system's future.

Many meteorologists are realizing that relying on computers to scan and summarize the abundant (or even excessive) information that piles up so quickly today is problematic because it distances them from personal familiarity with an area's weather and climate. More of them are reportedly returning to the old practice of preparing their own weather maps by hand to improve their forecasts. In fact, personal involvement in forecasting seems to be enjoying a renaissance. It is seen as a way to renew the fight against "meteorological cancer," a term coined in 1977 by meteorology pioneer Leonard Snellman to describe the professionally stultifying condition of being nothing more than a passive conduit for information generated by computers.

Take this lesson to heart: Rather than confining the search for variables to data depositories and getting lost in the numbers, you should begin the model-building process by reading books and articles by reputable historians of your field. Fortunately, good historians are often good forecasters. They develop a keen understanding of hard-to-measure forces that have shaped a system in the past and are skilled at using this knowledge to describe possible futures. Historians pay close attention to data and often use statistics to study cause and effect, but their final crystal ball views are as likely to be shaped by nonquantifiable variables like diplomatic activities, political transformations, scientific discoveries, technological advancements, environmental disasters, and social and cultural shifts.

Footnotes and reading lists in these publications will often help you identify current authorities on forces shaping the realm of possibilities for your system. Go ahead and call those authorities; in my experience, specialists can help with variable selection and often engage you in stimulating discussions.

Last, but definitely not least, have confidence in your own insights as an industry insider. You might know more about your system than any published expert, especially if you have been involved in it for many years. Do not be afraid to include a personally selected variable or two in your forecast model if you believe that others have failed to understand how things really work in your system. You may well be right, and if not, you can always revise or remove those variables when you periodically review your model. Here are two examples of the overall approach:

Example 5.1: Explanatory Variables for Undergraduate Education Model

Higher education has had its ups and downs in recent years, so what variables might be used to forecast the future for 4-year degree programs? Here are examples of explanatory variables that could be considered before the final cut is made:

- *Affordability*: Tuition would not be a valid variable because students pay so many different rates, including nothing if they have a full scholarship. Proxy variables might be created from per student cash payments and the present-discounted value of loan payments.
- *Opportunity costs*: College enrollment is known to vary with the employment rate and wages; students are more likely to work toward a degree when the alternative prospects for good-paying work are poor. Relative time commitment may also shed some light, especially as more colleges provide online education that allows students to be employed at the same time.
- *Comparative return on investment* (ROI): Enrollment decisions may be influenced by perceptions of employment following graduation. Demand for degrees will likely decline, for example, if nongraduates can make as much money as graduates.
- *Number of high school graduates*: An increase in high school dropouts would likely reduce the demand for undergraduate programs awarding a baccalaureate degree (and vice versa).
- *Ethnic mix in target market*: College attendance varies somewhat by ethnic background. Changes in immigration could have a significant impact on college enrollment.
- *Growth of alternative paths to high-skill jobs*: Given that some of the wealthiest young Americans did not go to college, the availability of entrepreneurial alternatives might be a growing influence on demand for undergraduate degrees. The "hack your education" movement might be a viable alternative.

Other variables will likely be described by research articles in higher education journals. However, the best variables might actually be identified via focus group interviews with students and prospective students; they are, after all, the ones making the decisions that will cause future demand for 4-year degrees to decline, stay the same, or increase.

Example 5.2: Explanatory Variables for Professional Services Model

Attorneys, accountants, lawyers, and other guild professionals probably have good reason to wonder about the future of their professions. Several changes in their marketplaces suggest that predictions based on past historical demand are particularly misleading. For example, articles in business publications report that clients are upset with high fees and low-quality work. Some new noneconomic variables will surely be needed to support a meaningful forecast, among them:

- *Regulatory environment*: Increases in government rules and regulations are important determinants of the future, probably increasing demand. However, deregulation and self-regulation would have opposite effects, creating the need for a careful analysis of the net effect over the forecast period.
- *Alternatives to professional services*: Compliance with many regulatory requirements can be automated, with a future impact proportional to ongoing development of viable software. Also, demand is likely to fall if regulatory enforcement becomes weak or penalty payments are less than the costs of compliance.
- *Redefinition of professional services*: The future of the demand for guild professionals might change substantially if they were to develop new financial and service relationships with their clients. Some evidence suggests demand is created when professionals go at risk with clients, that is, they shift from fee-for-service billing to gain-sharing.

These examples reinforce the need to evaluate futures with both objective and subjective analysis—forecasting. Data-driven predictive models could not incorporate some of the new, unmeasurable factors that are clearly going to decide the fate of 4-year colleges and professional service firms.

How to Specify the Model

Specification might be the most important step in forecasting: It expresses your artistic style and helps improve the accuracy and value of your forecasts. The first task is to reduce your complete list of explanatory variables to a methodologically appropriate number. Forecasters who select the most powerful explanatory variables—powerful in the sense of collectively shaping future possibilities—will be positioned to make the best forecasts, assuming accurate data and unbiased analysis. For example, I believe I am the only health futurist who includes medical science as a forecasting variable, which helps explain my success in forecasting several significant changes that others initially missed (e.g., the accelerating shift from inpatient acute care to outpatient management of chronic conditions).

After selecting five or fewer variables for in-depth analysis, you are ready to specify the future outcomes to be reported in your forecast, that is, the realm of possibilities to which probabilities will be assigned after the variables are analyzed. In meteorology, these are water, wind, and so on. Suggesting analogous possibilities for forecasts in all other systems would be impossible here, but a general approach can be adapted to fit the relevant outcomes in manufacturing, finance, technology, transportation, government, and the like.

A forecast generally encompasses the continuum of outcomes from negative to positive. In its simplest and perfectly useful form, a forecast estimates the probabilities of less, the same amount, or more of the selected measure of a dynamic system's future (e.g., financial performance, sales of goods and services). In more general terms, probabilities can be assigned to the possibilities of things getting worse, staying the same, or getting better for the system. For example, a forecast for new residential construction over the coming year might be expressed as a 20% likelihood that housing starts will decline with respect to the current year, a 30% chance they will stay the same, and a 50% chance they will increase. A forecast for employment over the coming year might be a 25% chance of decline, a 45% chance of no change from the current level, and a 30% chance of increase.

Note that a prediction would give only one specific value in each instance, such as a 3.5% increase in new residential construction or a 1.8% increase in employment. Some predictive models would generate absolute numbers, such as 823,000 new houses or 1,230,000 new jobs. These absolute numbers are often converted into relative measures to indicate *percentage* change.

If the future cannot be meaningfully represented on a continuous scale, discrete outcomes can be used to define the realm of possibilities. For example, my current forecast for the future of the Patient Protection and Affordable Care Act (ACA) assigns probabilities to five outcomes for health reform: ObamaCare being implemented as enacted by Congress, being implemented but not as enacted, being repealed, being neither implemented nor repealed, plus a GOK (God only knows) outcome such as invalidation by the Supreme Court in response to a new appeal. Each outcome has a distinctly different implication for a health care provider.

My 2- to 5-year forecast for health care businesses assigns probabilities to four possibilities: some form of financial failure (e.g., reorganization, liquidation, acquisition); survival without growth; thriving with growth; and a GOK development such as transition into another line of business. The probabilities are not presented here because they are frequently updated due to unpredictable events and climate change.

The final specification task is defining the time frame for the forecast. As a mathematical extrapolation from historical data, a prediction can be extended indefinitely into the future, but forecasts are issued for a finite period. You must decide the relevant time frame in advance and select a cutoff point when estimates of the probabilities move into the realm of pure speculation. For example, few meteorologists extend their local area forecasts beyond 5 days, and the accuracy of successive day-by-day forecasts even within a 5-day period declines over time. Long-range forecasters tend to be researchers who are constantly seeking to improve the process, but their progress is thwarted by global climate change.

Forecasts can be limited to a few months or quarters in highly volatile situations, such as estimates of stock values and gasoline prices. A reasonable time frame in most systems is a few years; this varies by system and can be expected to get shorter as the world becomes more complicated. I have been issuing viable 2- to 5-year forecasts in health care for several decades now, but the view in my crystal ball is starting to become pretty fuzzy beyond 3 years. I absolutely refuse to forecast beyond 5 years; that is entering the realm of science fiction in health care or just about any other dynamic system. For example, the government's 2010 prediction of the number of people with health insurance in 2019 is a pure SWAG (silly wild ass guess), as was its 2010 prediction of complete economic recovery by 2014.

How to Measure the Explanatory Variables

If you only remember one thing about measurement from the previous chapter, let it be this: Meaningful and accurate views of the future cannot be produced from meaningless or inaccurate data. GIGO (garbage in, garbage out) is a universal rule. This advice should suffice with respect to quantitative measurements (e.g., bushels of corn, on-time departures, hits on a website) that are loaded into a crystal ball.

Qualitative information in forecasting must be just as valid (meaningful) and reliable (accurate), but it also requires you to make subjective value judgments. For example, the future of economic growth is heavily dependent on congressional action (or inaction, in today's political climate). The federal budget's balance between fiscal and monetary policy would normally be an essential variable in a gross domestic product (GDP) forecasting model, but it cannot be objectively quantified. Further, at the time of this writing, the U.S. Congress is as likely to maintain current austerity as it is to cut budgets further or to create new stimulus programs. So, you will have to make up your own mind about economic and political measures if they are important to your sphere of influence. The only certain thing is that nothing is certain, another reason why forecasting's time has come.

To assign probabilities to the possibilities, you can draw on a wide range of perspectives from pundits, journalists, professors, researchers, think tank analysts, and so on. But, be careful: Many of their views reflect personal politics or their employers' political orientation; the pictures in their crystal balls are painted to reinforce that point of view, often in hopes of creating a self-fulfilling prophecy. What forecasting requires is unbiased interpretation of unbiased observations. Good forecasters suppress any desire to select or interpret information for the purpose of reaching a predetermined outlook.

Further, no objective data or subjective observations should be used simply because they are available. Initial information and its subsequent transformations need to be scrubbed of any bias before being included in a forecast that is going to be used for realistic decision making. For example, data from surveys can be biased (deliberately or not) in many ways, such as poorly worded questions, cleverly worded questions that exclude all but one possible response, nonrandom sampling, and low response rates.

You may actually need to create one or more explanatory variables on occasion. For example, a composite of several leading economic indicators might be constructed to prevent specification error, or the results of a series of focus group interviews might be transformed into an index that suggests future possibilities. I use both these approaches in my current model for forecasting the future of health care. For one of the five variables in my model, I combine objective government economic data with subjective surveys of patients' attitudes to create a subjective proxy for consumer medical spending power. My goal is to understand how consumers can and likely will respond to the accelerating shift from third-party reimbursement to individual responsibility for paying medical bills. This payment variable is one of the most powerful determinants of the future of health care, in my opinion, but it must be created and its magnitude estimated because it is unprecedented.

How to Analyze Variations over Time

After selecting the four or five most powerful explanatory variables and identifying sources of good information about them, you are almost ready to start forecasting. There is just one more preliminary step: evaluating each variable's expected contributions to changes in your dynamic sector. Predictive models generally have a built-in mathematical mechanism for ranking each variable's contributions to the future state, but the ranking must be done subjectively in forecasting. One or two variables will usually have more influence than the others, which means that their impact needs to be given more weight in the final forecast.

Several recent books, most prominently Nate Silver's *The Signal and the Noise* (New York: Penguin Press, 2012; and others identified at the end of the previous chapter), have addressed the importance of this step. The authors do a good job showing how predictions tend to fail because they do not incorporate real-world probabilities in their computations. Silver promoted a less-common approach, one based on Bayesian statistics, and demonstrated how it leads to better predictions by updating probabilities based on actual experience rather than retaining probabilities based on experiments (e.g., the standard Fisher approach to statistical analysis). By practicing what he preaches, Silver has developed an impressive model for using previous election results to define the realm of possibilities for future elections.

However, the Bayesian improvement still does not overcome all the real-world problems with predictions. In an election, for example, the statistically favored candidate might commit a fatal gaffe. Bad weather in a few precincts could create an upset. Unforeseen "swift-boating" can turn the tide of public opinion at the last minute. Ballot problems occasionally cause people to cast a vote opposite of what they intended. Last, but not least, a single justice on the Supreme Court can make the final vote irrelevant. None of these game-changing forces will be reflected in the data or included in the computation of the prediction. Each unquantifiable variable is rare in itself, but collectively they often decide elections. Using Bayesian statistics to make predictions is a good step in the right direction, but it does not cover all the territory. Forecasting does.

The Supreme Court decision on the ACA (June 28, 2012) is a good case in point. Intrade, a market mechanism that uses Bayesian concepts to update probabilities in real time, *predicted* the day before the ruling that the Supreme Court would overturn the mandate to purchase health insurance. I *forecasted* a 30% chance the mandate would be upheld, a 30% chance it would be rejected, and a 40% chance the decision would be a GOK surprise (neither outright approval nor complete rejection). I explained this forecast to several journalists who asked for my prediction before the decision, but I do not think any of them included it in their stories. They wanted a black-or-white answer, and the image in my crystal ball was gray.

My "surprise" forecast is turning out to be correct. A majority of justices upheld the mandate to purchase insurance but overruled ObamaCare's other linchpin, the requirement that states must expand Medicaid. The split decision, which was not a predicted outcome, created unintended consequences that now cast the entire law's future in question. Stock market analysts who initially took the Supreme Court ruling as a reason to buy health care stocks are having second thoughts as of this writing. For a variety of reasons, implementation is not living up to expectations.

Assigning Weight

As already noted, ranking variables to estimate the probabilities of several possibilities is a subjective process. A big part of a good forecaster's art is deciding how much weight to assign to each variable. Doing this well is usually a function of personal experience and understanding the lessons of history. The more time forecasters have spent in a dynamic system, the more meaningful their sense of the relative explanatory power of the variables. Of course, even the experienced forecaster must always be looking for climate changes that call for the forecaster to respecify the model, not to mention repeatedly asking what can possibly go wrong and what new things might happen.

The historical review you used to help you select your model's variables can also help you weight them. For example, the bitter debate between proponents of balanced budgets on the one hand and debt-financed stimulus on the other is deeply rooted in each side's different reading of economic history. Fiscal conservatives would expect long-run economic growth to be more likely when debt is reduced below a defined threshold. Liberals would see increasing debt as the most important variable for generating a return to sustained growth under current circumstances. Each camp's implicit forecasts are largely defined by the weight assigned to debt. (Without taking sides, I note that both camps are being forced to defend the accuracy and relevance of the data they use to make their projections.)

Relative ranking may also vary over time. For example, advancement in medical science is the most powerful variable in my health care forecast model, but its influence is strongest toward the end of the forecast period. The model's most powerful short-run factor is consumer medical spending power. In other words, the future of health care in my model is shaped more by consumer economics in the first and second years and more by revolutionary changes in medical science in the third year and beyond. The three other variables in my current model—information and communications technology, population health (the dynamics and demography of disease), and government health policy—each have the same weight over time and fit between the economic and scientific forces that trade places midway into the forecast period.

Studying the history of previous predictions and forecasts is another productive approach to weighting variables. A forecaster can learn a lot by reviewing what went right and what went wrong with previous gazes into the crystal ball. Why, for example, did nearly all futurists fail to foresee the sudden collapse of the technology bubble? How could so many miss the impending crash of 2008? How did a few contrarians get these things right? Or, were the contrarians just lucky?

Forecasters should also look back at their own forecasts and see why their projections were good or bad. Reweighting the variables is often the way to improve forecasting models. (I have a very good batting average in terms of *what* will happen, but I tend to jump the gun on *when.* Practicing what I preach, I am constantly trying to figure out why things often occur more slowly than expected and how to adjust my forecasts accordingly.)

How to Assemble the Forecast

Assembling forecasts is the final expression of a forecaster's skill and style. It is ultimately an individual process, fine-tuned over the years in response to cumulative experience and new knowledge. My interviews with meteorologists and review of the literature about forecasting models preparatory to writing this book revealed not only variation in individual approaches at any given time but also consensus that any individual weather forecaster's approach evolves over time. Becoming a good forecaster is a never-ending task—a challenge that should help novices overcome their fear of getting started because learning by doing is the only way to move forward.

You should also be emboldened by the fact that meteorologists do not all start with the same step-by-step process. If there were a single model that all forecasters had to learn and follow, forecasting would have a standard examination for professional licensure, such as the certified public accountant (CPA) or bar exams—and it would be the core concept in this chapter. This is decidedly not the case. There is no substitute for learning the basic principles of forecasting, starting to forecast, and expecting to develop a personal approach based on trial and error over time. That is what meteorologists do.

Consensus forecasting provides an excellent foundation for getting started. The process includes gathering predictions or forecasts from a number of respected analysts and then estimating (yes, deciding for yourself) the central tendency of their collective thinking. As you may remember if you took statistics, central tendency can be measured three different ways: mean (average), median (midpoint), and mode (most common). Part of the consensus forecaster's art is developing a personalized approach to measuring central tendency and the distribution of variations around it, then deciding how to merge it with their own analysis.

If you go with consensus forecasting, you must also decide, *before* you start the process, what to do with outliers. The range of views about a specific dynamic system's future can be pretty wide. Eliminating extreme values is common, but I do not recommend this practice and therefore will not tell you how it is done—especially because the few correct predictions in recent years have tended to be the outliers.

The general process for assembling a consensus forecast consists of four steps:

■ First, *decide which projections to include.* You will need to find others' forecasts and predictions that are directly relevant to your dynamic system. The search should normally be confined to projections for comparable geographic and product markets or industry classifications (including nonprofit and government). The use of forecasts and predictions from other countries (think other climates) is seldom appropriate and would need to be justified by special circumstances. You may also need to obtain legal authorization to use information from third-party sources, especially when the data are proprietary and sold by subscription. You will want to explicitly exclude input from analysts with known biases or bad track records, even if it is available without restrictions or costs.

■ Second, *decide how to standardize measurements.* Analysts are not required to make their forecasts and predictions in a consistent format, which means that you may have to convert the information you collect to a common scale. (You can read how to do this conceptually in a basic statistics textbook; it is the underlying concept of the standard deviation.) For example, some projections will be stated in absolute terms, such as dollars to be spent on a specific category of goods or services, and some will be stated as relative changes in future spending; it is up to you to pick the one you want to use. You will also need to standardize time frames to the extent possible, so that the consensus forecast is made for an identifiable period. Treating 1-year and 5-year forecasts as comparable is like comparing apples and oranges.

■ Third, *decide how to weight the collected projections.* Weighting others' future assessments is not absolutely necessary, but some inputs will obviously be worth more than others. For example, if one forecaster has been right twice as often as another, you might give that person's projection twice the weight when you assemble the consensus. Projections based on large, good samples often deserve more weight than those based on only a few observations, and analyses based on data collected specifically for the future assessment could be worth more than analyses using secondary data collected for other purposes.

■ Fourth, *consider what could go wrong in the dynamic system.* Adhering to the basic types of weather forecasting models—consensus, ensemble, or ingredients based— does not automatically bring in the element of uncertainty that makes forecasting superior to predicting in most systems. Estimates of the probabilities of very remote but consequential possibilities (e.g., black swans) or totally unprecedented game-changing outcomes (e.g., GOK events) are never included in predictions and not often enough in forecasts. But, recent experience suggests that uncommon and unprecedented possibilities are starting to occur much more often.

Forecasters put their personal stamp on a forecast by deciding (1) how to manage or modify this basic, four-step assembling process; and (2) whether to add a GOK component (which I strongly advocate when the possibilities are not confined by a continuous scale). Individual style also evolves as a result of ongoing participation in forecast discussion groups. I recommend that new futurists become involved in discussions with other futurists as much as possible. Professional associations could serve a useful purpose by organizing discussion forums for members who want to look in a crystal ball or judge the work of those who do it for them. (Indeed, industry organizations could do a lot to help their members by promoting the art of forecasting.)

From Weather to Whether

If you still doubt that forecasting is just as much art as science, check out Chicago's two very good forecasting sources: the National Oceanic and Atmospheric Administration's National Weather Service (NOAA/NWS; http://www.weather.gov), and WGN-TV/Chicago Tribune meteorologist Tom Skilling (http://www.chicagoweathercenter.com), who has a team of weather experts working for him. Both review the same scientific data and quantitative models several times every day.

And yet, their forecasts tend to vary markedly, reflecting differences in subjective assessments of the data and consensus discussions within their teams. On any given day, one of their forecasts is usually closer to the actual weather where I live near downtown Chicago, but the opposite can be true in the suburbs. I cannot say that one group is better than the other; their results seem to be comparable over time. Like physicians' diagnoses, their forecasts are professionally constructed but sometimes wrong. In any case, it is nice to have a second opinion.

"Perhaps you'd like a second opinion?"

Although forecasting is not yet common outside the realm of weather, it has been successfully practiced for many years in a few other fields:

■ Blue Chip Economic Indicators (BCEI; www.bluechippubs. com) is widely recognized for its consensus forecasts on national and global economies. (Full disclosure: My father's cousin, Robert Eggert, founded Blue Chip at about the time I was transitioning from weather to economics. I took full advantage of Bob's insights into the differences between predicting and forecasting when we got together at family reunions.)

■ Nate Silver's regular column and blog for the *New York Times*, FiveThirtyEight (http://fivethirtyeight.blogs.nytimes. com) focuses on elections but covers an interesting mix of other political and economic subjects as well.

■ Problem Knowledge Couplers (PKC; http://www.pkc. com), is a forecasting tool that helps health profession- als reach a diagnosis by presenting the evidence-based range of possible disorders and diseases for a specific set of signs and symptoms.

BCEI, FiveThirtyEight, and PKC all do a good job integrat- ing narrow predictions into broad forecasts for refinement by humans with extensive experience in their respective domains. As we have already seen, soundly formulated predictions can be valuable inputs for forecasting; good forecasters use them selectively as one of several resources for defining the realm of possibilities and probabilities. For example, I study lots of predictions about the future of health care before I look in my crystal ball, but my final forecast is always more expansive than any of the predictions. It may lack the seeming precision of a single-outcome prediction, but it provides a much more realistic outlook because—all together now—the future has many more possibilities.

Before explaining strategy's power to shape better futures from possibility-rich forecasts in the next chapter, I leave the last word to a prominent meteorologist, C. A. Doswell, who has been at the center of the long-standing debate between scientists who think computers alone can predict the weather and more traditional forecasters who believe that humans must still be involved in the process. Leaders making decisions in other dynamic systems should see his point as one more rea- son to join the forecasting team.

It is axiomatic that the best forecasters base their forecasts on knowledge of the atmosphere by apply- ing models of the atmosphere. That those models are not always "objective" does not mean they are without value. If a forecaster learns continually from experience, from scientific journals, from colleagues, or whatever … those forecasters are acting as scientists whether they recognize it or not.

We cannot afford to turn our backs on important knowledge simply because it is non-quantitative or subjective. In fact, it is the integration of diverse data and abstract knowledge which humans are so good at and which is so hard to teach a computer since the synthesis is not totally quantitative. At best, the human diagnostic process is capable of success far beyond that of automated objectivity. ("The Human Element in Weather Forecasting," *National Weather Digest* 11(2):7, 1986)

Chapter 6

From Forecasts to Strategies

> Everybody talks about the weather, but nobody does anything about it.

—Mark Twain (or Charles Dudley Warner?)

This book began by proposing to end the common practice of using *predicting* and *forecasting* as synonyms. I argued that treating them as different words to describe a single prognostic process robs us of the power to envision better outcomes—potentially compromising our futures. However, this book will not accomplish its ultimate goal if it does not take you beyond "talking about the weather" (i.e., the future) of your own dynamic system. This final chapter therefore explains how to translate your new knowledge about forecasting the future into actually doing something about it.

Here, again, predictions fall down on the job: They do not provide directions for doing anything other than passively waiting. As a statement of what will happen at a specific time, a prediction does not convey actionable information about alternatives to consider—and which ones to pursue. It is a take-it-or-leave-it proposition, essentially: no hard choices, no fork in the road ahead (so unlike the real world).

Predictions are not motivating, either, for a paradoxical reason: A prediction shows where things are headed, with an appearance of precision, but experience suggests you have no reason to believe it. Why bother responding when the future will almost certainly turn out to be something else? Given that predictions usually do not foretell the future any better than the flip of a coin, doing nothing in response is as defensible as doing something. A prediction of something bad would potentially initiate defensive action, but the idea of influencing a prediction's possibilities—effectively going on offense—is not part of the picture.

A forecast, in contrast, is energizing and empowering. Its essential plurality, the probabilities of possibilities, implies choices to be made. A forecast tells us not only that different outcomes are possible and, to varying degrees, likely, but that several different possibilities can occur simultaneously within

"And so, extrapolating from the best figures available, we see that current trends, unless dramatically reversed, will inevitably lead to a situation in which the sky will fall."

the area and time it covers. The absence of implied certainty is itself a motivating factor; things might not be all that bad or all that good—which means you may be able to affect the outcome. The possibility of going in more than one direction suggests the efficacy of planning ahead, which is why, after many years of experience with both ways of looking into a crystal ball, I believe forecasting should replace predicting in dynamic systems.

Let us look at the proactive process of planning using alternatives revealed by forecasting, followed by a discussion of responsive actions to influence the future—forecasting's "magic sauce" that is not found in half-baked predictions. The chapter concludes by defining strategy and showing how strategic planning can be used to accomplish the shift from predicting to forecasting.

Expecting Multiple Outcomes

The switch to forecasting will spare us one of predicting's most opportunity-crushing consequences: creating a single picture of the future. For example, a prediction of a bull market creates the impression that stock prices are going to go up. In actuality, the Dow Jones Industrial Average (already identified in Chapter 3 as a flawed representation of the stock market) may rise, but the number of declining shares could easily exceed gainers for the period covered by the prediction. A prediction of falling prices for crude petroleum suggests that the cost of gasoline will soon follow suit, completely overlooking the fact that prices at the pump will likely rise in states with refinery problems and tax increases, while falling in anti-tax states with excess refining capacity.

Or, consider a government-predicted decline in unemployment. It will surely be heralded by media as a sign that employers will start hiring again—which may be the case in hurricane-ravaged coastal areas that start receiving insurance payments and federal disaster relief, but quite the opposite is likely to happen in rust-belt states where employers are pushing existing workers to increase productivity rather than hiring new ones.

Another example is the predicted end of a company that has no future because its core product is obsolete or its management inept. As a Chicagoan, I can immediately think of several local corporations that recently defied premature predictions of their demise by moving successfully in directions not represented in the data used to make the original predictions, such as Kraft and Motorola each splitting into two companies and McDonald's changing its menu and franchise arrangements.

Speaking of Chicago, the problem is reflected in the name of a nationally famous radio show that started here, "The Rest of the Story." Commentator Paul Harvey delighted in revisiting old media reports that turned out to have taken a new and different twist once all the details were reported. His retelling always showed that the story was not as simple as it originally seemed. The same is true of predictions.

A preoccupation with getting simple (i.e., oversimplified) answers is embedded in the questions journalists tend to ask us futurists: Is the stock market going to continue rising? Will hospitals stay in business when the insurance mandate kicks in? How long will housing prices stay low? Can Apple survive without Steve Jobs? Is this the China century? Will drought destroy the farm belt? Will student debt create a new recession? Will Republicans regain the Senate in 2014? Will the Cubs win the World Series? (Just kidding.) I long for the day when a reporter calls instead to ask what are the options and what are the chances.

Today, just about everyone wants a yes or no (a prediction), but the only meaningful answer is that it depends (a forecast), and that things could go in any of several directions—all at the same time. In other words, do not stay out of the stock market just because predictions say it will go up or down. Rather, look at a forecast with probabilities for declining, steady, and increasing stocks. Then, evaluate the independent variables that explain the three different outcomes and buy or sell accordingly. Some investors already follow this forecast-oriented approach, but many more miss opportunities or make mistakes because they act on predictions.

The same insistence on yes/no where maybe is the best answer can be seen in views about the post-reform future of hospitals. Some industry analysts are predicting a "train wreck" as third-party reimbursement declines over the next few years, while others predict hospitals will be better off due to a higher number of patients with insurance. After looking in my crystal ball, I forecast that 30% of all hospitals will fail in their current business model (i.e., liquidate, reorganize, or be acquired at a loss); 45% will "get by" (i.e., maintain a zero margin by keeping costs in line with declining revenues); and 25% will experience impressive growth by proactively changing their business models to reflect shifts in medical science, payment, technology, demographics, and health policy.

The futures of housing, personal electronics, China, agriculture, and every other dynamic system are subject to just as many simultaneous possibilities, from bad to good, for reasons that could range from business as usual to uncommon or even unprecedented events. Sadly, forecasting does not allow us to pick one option from the many. But, it does remind us that the future is unpredictable and diverse, that several different outcomes are possible, and that we may want to prepare for all of them—that is, finding the organizational equivalent of wearing layered clothing, carrying an umbrella, and packing waterproof boots because we might need them all on a day with a 40% chance of rain or snow. Or, we can decide to stay home or move to Phoenix.

Victoria Roberts

*"I can't seem to live in the present, you don't want me to
live in the past, so I'm opting for the future as I see it."*

Happily, a forecast offers those in many dynamic systems
another option: trying to influence probabilities to push the
future in a desired direction.

Creating the Future from the Forecast

Forecasters have worked for over a century to understand
atmospheric physics well enough to change the weather
through intervention in its processes. Seeding clouds to create rain over dry farmland is a well-known example of
this practice; banning aerosol cans is another. Still another
was the research project in which I learned weather

forecasting—finding ways to prevent the formation of damaging hailstones, such as increasing pressure or temperature within clouds. (The project actually found solutions, but their secondary effects were more damaging than the hail they prevented.)

Forecasters in other dynamic systems can likewise consider active intervention, once they understand the causal variables and their interactions. Some variables in a forecast model probably cannot be manipulated for purposes of changing the outcomes, but a few might be subject to acceptable manipulation, such as initiating a targeted information campaign to prepare health care consumers for their new responsibilities or starting a creatively destructive business in a shopworn market sector.

Seeing opportunities to shift the probabilities of possibilities in a desirable way is the hallmark of visionary, ethical leaders in business, government, social movements, education, entertainment—pretty much any dynamic system you can think of. It already defines the work of lobbyists and publicists. (Of course, we as a society need to be on the alert for illegal or uneconomical interventions to influence the future. Many business executives, politicians, and government officials deserve to be behind bars for behind-the-scenes efforts to jigger the future for personal gain.)

Innovative Intervention

Property and casualty insurance companies need to forecast payouts for damage caused by natural disasters as part of their rate-setting process. Predicting future claims based solely on past experience does not make sense in this particularly dynamic system; hazardous weather is occurring more frequently, and our growing population is occupying more land. These unprecedented changes would suggest a tendency toward increased future payouts, but on the other hand, factors such as weather's cyclical patterns and declining property values in areas most frequently affected by storms would suggest stable claims. Yet other possibilities, such as abandonment of storm-prone areas and more people deciding to "go bare" (i.e., taking their chances without insurance), would suggest a future reduction in claims. And, indeed, all these divergent changes are taking place now, reinforcing the case for forecasting.

This three-outcome forecast reveals several opportunities for interventions to influence future claims and thus profitability. Although carriers could not affect climate change within the forecast's time frame, they could put more emphasis on charging special rates for structures incorporating storm-resistant designs (as electric utilities have done for energy-efficient homes). They could also work with local and state governments to prevent rebuilding in vulnerable areas. They might even create the property and casualty equivalent of a whole-life policy, which builds value for beneficiaries over time while allowing withdrawals when needed.

Finally, a casualty company might create prevention and mitigation programs for policyholders, such as arranging discounts on storm-resistant storage safes or setting up cell phone alerts of impending weather events with reminders of last-minutes steps to avoid or reduce damage. (In the same way, health insurance companies are starting to provide direct assistance to their most expensive beneficiaries—those with manageable chronic diseases.) Innovative property and casualty insurers have already begun to take some of these steps, possibly without realizing they are already approaching the future as forecasters.

Forecasting has another important implication for the future of organizations that sell something: careful selection of customers. The usual goal of improving market share will not lead to success when customers are heading in at least three different directions and one of them is insolvency. The common sales practice of qualifying leads can keep companies from wasting time on potential customers unlikely to make a purchase (e.g., the prospect just purchased a competitor's product or already allocated its budget for the coming year). However, your business will be worse off if it closes deals with customers who cannot pay their bills in the future. If I am correct in forecasting that 30% of all hospitals will fail financially in 3 to 5 years, suppliers will want to evaluate their potential hospital clients carefully to maximize their chances of selling to the other 70%. In this way, forecasting adds a preventive dimension to strategy and planning.

Strategic Planning

My first exposure to concepts of strategic planning occurred 40 years ago as I was starting the research for my doctoral dissertation in economics. Because I was studying how doctors managed their practices, my thesis adviser urged me to read a brand new book by Peter Drucker, *Management: Tasks, Responsibilities, Practices* (New York: HarperCollins, 1973). Drucker's definition of strategic planning is timeless:

> Strategic planning is the continuous process of making present entrepreneurial *(risk-taking) decisions* systematically and with the greatest knowledge of

their futurity; organizing systematically the *efforts*
needed to carry out these decisions; and measuring
the results of these decisions against the expectations
through organized, *systematic feedback.* [All italics in
original text.]

Strategic planning's link to forecasting is obvious; Drucker's
references to systems thinking and knowledge of futurity reso-
nate perfectly with a future expressed as probabilities of possibilities. The explicit extension of these concepts to "entrepreneurial
(*risk-taking*) *decisions*" is also congruent with a central premise
of this book. For example, Drucker surely felt that senior executives compromised the future of the automobile industry because
industry leaders did not take risks. Their failure to see the substantially different strategic implications of selling versus marketing led them into a false sense of security, which gave foreign
manufacturers an open door to the U.S. marketplace.

Ironically, Peter Drucker's definition of strategic planning
was preceded by the assertion that *"strategic planning is not
forecasting."* He goes on to treat predicting and forecasting
as synonyms throughout the rest of the section, but he concludes by arguing that *"strategic planning is absolutely necessary precisely because* we cannot be certain about the future"
[italics his]. It seems clear that Drucker would have appreciated
the power of forecasting had he understood the difference
between it and predicting.

Strategic planning quickly took hold in both private and
public sectors. It was the topic of many best-selling books
throughout the 1970s and 1980s. Consulting firms made mil-
lions developing strategic plans for companies and government
agencies. Strategic planning was even the cornerstone of a
major health reform law passed the year I started my career as
a medical school professor, the National Health Planning and
Resources Development Act of 1974. Indeed, the law made my

job possible by providing grants for academic health centers to teach economics to health care's future decision makers.

My first professorial assignment was to develop a course in strategic planning because the new law required health care providers to submit strategic plans to receive a certificate of need (i.e., a government authorization to build more hospital beds and purchase new equipment). The medical school's curriculum guidelines required me to define key terms in the course syllabus. Peter Drucker provided the classic definition of strategic planning, but not of strategy. Being one of the first professors to teach strategic planning in a medical school, I had to define the basic concept on my own and contrast it with the prevalent practice of day-to-day management.

Strategy versus Tactics

Here is the definition that has worked well for me over the past four decades:

Strategy: a purposeful response to anticipated changes, consistent with the organization's mission and values

The word *purposeful* establishes the imperative to define responses *before* anticipated changes occur rather than in reaction to them. The reference to an organization's mission and values sets important conditions on strategy. For example, because their objectives are different, a for-profit chain hospital and a tax-exempt community hospital would be expected to develop some different strategies in response to the same forecast: The proprietary hospital would aim to make a profit for its shareholders; the community hospital would put top priority on taking care of anyone who came through the doors. (Mission and values are themselves occasionally affected by a forecast, as seen in the step some nonprofit hospitals are taking to convert to for-profit status in anticipation of expected changes in reimbursement and competition. That is a big strategic change, but taking care of anyone who walks through a hospital's doors will not keep the doors open in many communities.)

The role of the strategist is to look ahead, decide what changes can and should be made to align with future possibilities, and then to reallocate resources accordingly. Strategists focus on making big decisions, redirecting the enterprise in consideration of external changes that do not augur well for business as usual. One essential tool for performing this function is forecasting.

Directors of companies, board members of nonprofits, and legislators are all strategists. They are responsible for working with their chief executives to look ahead, decide how to rebalance the organization's goods and services, and then change production processes to meet the new goals. Likewise, strategists in the military must anticipate where wars are likely to start, determine how to deploy forces most effectively, and decide which weapons systems to acquire. In the commercial world, strategy can encompass product transition (replacing ice cream with "dairy desert" in anticipation of rising milk prices), business model redevelopment (dealerships starting to lease cars rather than sell them when buyers' incomes are not expected to keep up with rising costs of ownership), or totally reinventing a company (e.g., IBM's shift from manufacturing to consulting services in response to expected changes in the global economy), among many other possible responses.

Holding Leaders Responsible

Leaders responsible for an organization's long-run survival must be held accountable for integrating forecasts into strategic decision making. Exploring the probabilities of possibilities, evaluating a range of viable responses, and then defining specific strategies should be key criteria of chief executive performance review for any enterprise operating in a dynamic system—and reflected in executive compensation.

This is not a book about the long-term risks of investors' current fixation on short-term results, but I foresee many companies failing over the next few years because their executives have not looked beyond current profitability and shareholder value (and, of course, their own immediate compensation). The recommended shift from predicting to forecasting will help many companies avoid disaster by identifying new opportunities to harness. It should also help solve some of the larger systemic problems attributed to investors' demands for short-term gains at the expense of long-term survival and growth.

For day-to-day operations that keep enterprises in business while strategies are being considered, the appropriate set of management tools is called tactics. Like predicting and forecasting, strategy and tactics are not synonyms. *Merriam-Webster's Dictionary* provides a good functional definition of the latter:

Tactics: the art or skill of employing available means to accomplish an end

The key to tactics is employing *available* means. Good tacticians find the best combination of labor and materials on hand to ensure survival of the enterprise over the next day, week, or month. Because changes are not expected in these time periods, conditions are fixed. In both military and civilian settings, the tactician is the leader on the front lines, fighting the battles of the moment. The chief operating officer heads the tactical team, typically made up of managers. Good management theory says that the directors and chief executive should let them do their jobs (and, of course, replace them when they do not).

Time Dimensions of Strategy and Tactics

The time frames of strategy (traditionally called the long run) and tactics (the short run) should not be defined in the same calendar unit for all organizations. The once-common practice of linking strategy to a 5-year plan and tactics to annual budget cycles is now meaningless. The pace of change is uneven for any organization in today's chaotic environment, and it varies widely from system to system.

The strategic calendar also needs to incorporate an economic concept called *absorptive capacity*—a measure of an organization's capability to respond to change. To improve this measure, it is often necessary to assess and address corporate culture, which can be a major impediment. Why waste money on forecasting and strategy in an organization that is incapable of purposeful change, even when the future depends on it? (Fill in your own example here—I am surely not the only one who has worked in organizations where culture trumps strategy.) We can all think of companies that are in business today only because government bailouts saved them from the self-inflicted consequences of staying on their internally predicted path, oblivious to the realm of possibilities.

Leaders in every dynamic system need to evaluate organizational capacity to change as they establish an appropriate cycle for making forecasts and preparing strategies. Indeed, creating a culture of change may be a necessary first step in the process, possibly even a matter of life and death as political and economic environments become less forgiving. Special attention must be paid to the speed with which change can be accomplished in dynamic systems in which fast trumps big. (Surely the days of "too big to fail" are numbered.)

Assuming enough absorptive capacity, the strategic time frame is defined by the months or years needed to conduct an in-depth forecast, purposefully change direction, and then reallocate resources as necessary to accomplish the strategic change. This can be as short as a few quarters in high-tech businesses, such as cellular telephones; it can be a decade in capital-intensive, heavily regulated industries like electric power generation.

The health care sector is somewhere in between, in my opinion, with a strategic time frame from 2 to 5 years. Why? Most medical enterprises are incapable of making changes in less than 2 years (increasingly a threat to their survival), and 5 years is about as far ahead as anyone can reasonably anticipate new scientific, economic, and political forces that will shape the marketplace.

Basics of a Strategic Plan

Before ending this chapter, I must stress the importance of a strategic plan as the formal document that, in Drucker's words, causes the vision of a desired future "to degenerate into work." Many readers will have already been exposed to strategic plans in a class or at work, so this brief summary is designed to highlight the links between an effective plan and forecasting. (For those who need more information, several useful resources are identified in the "Additional Readings" section.)

A strategic plan is essential for reaping all the benefits of the shift from predicting to forecasting. Sadly, such documents are seldom written and implemented in today's world because so many businesses focus on surviving in the short run at the expense of thriving in the long run. Note that a strategic plan is different from the highly detailed business plan required of entrepreneurs seeking venture capital to *start* a business. Rather, it is a much more concise document that shapes decisions about the future for an existing enterprise.

Business plans often run over 100 pages and provide guidelines for tactical decisions; good strategic plans normally should not exceed 10 pages. The former is a blueprint for building a specific organizational structure; the latter provides instructions for leading an organization in an unstable system in a new, desired direction. (A strategic plan is not necessary for an enterprise in a stable system where the future is predictable—assuming that the enterprise is acceptably riding the trend.)

A basic strategic plan is a written document that includes the following information:

■ An executive-level summary of the forecast, sometimes called an environmental scan or list of opportunities and threats, that identifies the possibilities an organization is likely to encounter in its strategic time frame (i.e., the period beginning when resources can be reallocated to meet different goals and ending when informed analysis becomes wild speculation).

■ A rank-ordered list of the forecasted options that have been evaluated, with discussion of their potential implications for the organization and an honest assessment of the organization's ability to respond to them, including strengths and weaknesses. (Nominal group process techniques, weighted voting, and other methods for prioritizing the forecast elements can be found in "how-to" books on strategic planning processes.)

■ A feasible number of goals selected from the list of strategic possibilities, *measurable* performance objectives, and specific tasks to implement them. Note the words *feasible number*; most organizations are challenged to accomplish one major change a year (although several goals can be pursued simultaneously). A total of three or four goals is usually more than enough for a multiyear strategic plan.

■ A line-item budget that provides adequate resources to meet the goals and related objectives for purposefully changing the organization. Why go to all the trouble of forecasting and making plans if there will not be any money to implement the strategies? Leaders must resist the temptation to reduce or eliminate planning budgets when times are tough; after all, the purpose of forecasting and strategizing is to get to a better place.

■ Responsibility and authority for accomplishing each task; identifying specific personnel who have what it takes to get the jobs done. This is the stage of the process when plans degenerate into work, so strategic vision is no longer required. Staff assigned to these tasks are usually tacticians who are focused on using the budget and performance objectives (their "numbers") to make things happen.

■ A timeline that shows the starting and ending dates for each task required to implement the objectives, commonly presented as a task flow diagram or process chart with horizontal lines or boxes showing the task sequence. Several software packages are available to simplify this process; the best ones show the budget and personnel assignments for each task over the life of the planning cycle.

■ Appendices, if necessary, to present supportive charts, tables, and other essential information.

Condensing all this content into a short, focused, well-written document is a time-consuming task, but worth the effort. Keep in mind that the ultimate purpose of the strategic plan is to translate the forecast, with its opportunity-rich realm of possibilities, into specific actions that the organization will take to get where it wants to go while weathering the inevitable storms along the way. It is the guide for doing something about the weather—finding silver linings in black clouds.

Conclusion

Thanks for staying the course. We have come a long way together, beginning with striking assertions that predicting and forecasting are not synonyms, and that we often, and unnecessarily, pay a heavy price for failing to understand the difference. "What's the big deal?" was surely a common reaction at the start. I hope the answer is now obvious. And, I hope that you are motivated to start forecasting in your dynamic system and strategizing to create the best possible future from the realm of probabilities.

As we saw, predictive science has a long history dating back to Sir Isaac Newton's vision of a clockwork universe. His laws of nature and mathematical models to apply them have survived the test of time—in stable systems where quantifiable relationships that explained how things worked in the past continue to explain how they will work in the future. Predictions are appropriate for estimating a system's future states when history can be expected to repeat itself.

However, predictions have not done well where things are changing without historical precedent, where patterns are not repeating. Predictions also fail to foretell the future of dynamic systems in a useful way for other reasons, including intractable problems with models and data, and they divert decision makers from strategic innovations. The poor track record of predictions in economic, political, and social systems in the recent past suggests that we might as well use a random process to foretell the future. Yet, the accelerating rate of change in these systems suggests we have got to do better. We are robbing ourselves of good possibilities.

I became increasingly aware of predicting's limitations over a four-decade career as medical economist and health futurist. However, because I was trained in meteorology before economics, I realized over the years that the tools of weather forecasting were much better than those of economics for discerning the realm of possibilities in the medical marketplace, a dynamic system in which the future is definitely not a predictable extension of the past.

You have now seen how those forecasting tools can be used in other systems in which sophisticated analysis of data—even big data—cannot paint a complete picture of the future because it will be created, at least in part, by resources and forces that never existed before. You have also seen how strategic planning can help you reap the benefits of alternatives that can be forecasted but not predicted.

So, get started. Assess what could happen that has never happened before. Ask also what could possibly go wrong. Assign probabilities to the possibilities after analyzing all available information, engaging in consensus discussions, and following your own informed hunches. Then, decide what you can do (ethically and legally, of course) to create a desired outcome and write it up in a good strategic plan. Repeat the process as soon as the variables and climate change. I can guarantee you that the climate will change because we are increasingly surrounded by chaos.

> *chaos* [L, fr., Gk] 1) obs CHASM, GULF, ABYSS 2) a state of things in which chance is supreme 3) a state of utter confusion completely wanting in order: nature that is subject to no law or that is not necessarily uniform; especially *the confused unorganized state before the creation of distinctly organized forms.* (*Webster's New Collegiate Dictionary*)

But you can go beyond talking about the chaotic future to actually doing something about it. Look in your upgraded crystal ball and be a daring spirit.

> The whole body like a chaos capable of any form that the next daring spirit shall brood upon it.
>
> **—Selden, *The Laws of England,* quoted in *Oxford English Dictionary,* 2nd ed.**

Additional Readings

Many readers will already have a book or two on strategic planning from college days or graduate school. For those who want to update their resources, the following books are worthy of consideration: Olsen, Erica, *Strategic Planning for Dummies* (Hoboken, NJ: Wiley, 2012); Jakhotiya, Girish P., *Strategic Planning, Execution, and Measurement (SPEM): A Powerful Tool for CEOs* (New York: Productivity Press, 2013); Haines, Stephen, *The Systems Thinking Approach to Strategic Planning and Management* (New York: CRC Press, 2000); and Bryson, John M., *Strategic Planning for Public and Nonprofit Organizations: A Guide to Strengthening and Sustaining Organizational Achievement*, 4th edition (San Francisco: Jossey-Bass, 2011).

I strongly recommend two other books that I have assigned when teaching courses on strategy: Geisel, Theodor Seuss, *If I Ran the Zoo* (New York: Random House, 1950); and *On Beyond Zebra* (New York: Random House, 1955). Seriously, I do not know anyone better than Dr. Seuss for getting us to think about a new and better realm of possibilities.

Postscript: Big Data

I have written very little about "big data" so far, intentionally relegating this topic du jour to a postscript. I do not think it is directly relevant to explaining the consequential differences between forecasting and predicting. The ongoing expansion of capabilities to process data will influence our futures, but the new analytics does not necessarily create a better way for leaders to understand what those futures might be. For reasons already elaborated in the previous pages, the ability to process an ever-expanding body of *historical* information does not solve the problem of projecting future states for unstable systems. However, two related topics—big data and looking at the future, and the future of big data—are worth addressing.

Let me be clear on a key point: in minimizing big data's relevance for projecting long-run futures and making strategic decisions, I am not questioning its enormous tactical value for business and public policy. Big data is a big deal, and it will most likely get even bigger. This genie will not go back in the bottle. Leaders will continue to see dramatic growth in the quantity of raw data they can quickly transform into actionable information and, potentially, into knowledge and even wisdom (in terms of information science's DIKW hierarchy).

Big Data and Looking at the Future

A common definition of big data is still emerging, but its meaning seems to be converging around the integrated use of hardware and software to study measurements of what has happened within a system. It has a special focus on identifying patterns and behaviors that can be used to influence subsequent events. The usefulness of big data increases with the quantity of data, all other things being equal. Because the quantity of available data is increasing at a mind-boggling rate in almost every system, the depth and breadth of big data's reach are also expanding. John MacCormick provides a fascinating introduction to the technology behind this growth in *9 Algorithms that Changed the Future: The Ingenious Ideas that Drive Today's Computers* (Princeton: Princeton University Press, 2013).

New applications of big data are reported almost daily in the pages of the *Wall Street Journal* and the *New York Times*. For example, retail stores are boosting sales by positioning merchandise to reflect different consumers' paths through the aisles. Police departments are parsing incident reports to deploy officers where crimes are most likely to occur. Political campaigns are using analytics to identify undecided voters and target pitches directly to them. Advertisers are finding people most likely to purchase specific items and providing them with promotional incentives through personalized communications channels (e.g., direct mail, e-mail, social networks, even telephone calls). Online merchants are steering their customers toward products purchased by people with similar tastes and preferences. And so on.

The new analytical methods and practical applications are producing impressive results. As Viktor Mayer-Schonberger and Kenneth Cukier argue in their thoughtful book, *Big Data* (Boston: Eamon Dolan, 2013), the expanding capability to quantify correlations provides powerful insights into a system's dynamics. One of big data's hottest applications, predictive analytics, demonstrably helps organizations reduce costs and increase sales through a variety of responsive actions, such as performing maintenance just before breakdowns are most likely to occur or focusing attention on customers who can reasonably be expected to generate the highest marginal revenues. Decisions based on predictive analytics help explain how many businesses are currently making profits in a stagnant economy.

Still, predictive analytics does not explain everything. Mayer-Schonberger and Cukier appropriately note that the tools of big data are capable of determining with impressive precision what happens, but not why. They believe big data users will willingly sacrifice natural concern with causality in exchange for precise information about correlations. Most decision-makers will be so impressed with the nearly immediate gains from understanding correlation that they will overlook the risk of occasional losses from responding to random, meaningless patterns.

The methodological purist in me wants to disagree with their conclusion, but I am willing to accept it in the short-run (defined in Chapter 6 as the period when factors are fixed, which can vary between months and years on a system-specific basis). Knowing what happened without knowing why it happened can help leaders make good decisions—as long as why it happened doesn't change within the time frame in which responsive actions are taken.

In other words, correlations are very useful for guiding decisions while the *why* that explained them remains constant. Big data's potential to emulate a crystal ball fundamentally depends, therefore, on ongoing stability of the causal factors behind the correlations. That is, leaders can confidently use big data to make future-focused decisions in business and public policy as long as they have good reason to believe that the *why* behind the *what* is stable.

I've already had my say about instability in most systems in today's turbulent world. My acceptance of big data is correspondingly tempered by my belief that the past is less and less a good foundation for projecting futures. Big data's proponents need to be more openly attentive to this issue—recognizing that the value of correlations diminishes not over specific units of time like months or years, but over whatever time it takes for correlations to start having new explanations. Big data's influence on the future will depend on how sensitive its practitioners are to what might be called correlation relevance decay. They delude themselves and their clients if they try to foretell what will happen beyond that point. (Perhaps a "use by" date should be attached to data bases, with numbers being removed as soon as they have expired.)

There's another problem with expecting big data to become a futurist's tool. Predicting and forecasting are methods for assessing what and when (i.e., timing), not just what and maybe why. Time is always a variable in mathematical models for making predictions and forecasts, but big data formulas for finding relationships, other than plots of change in a single variable over time (the simplest form of prediction), do not include a time factor. As valuable as big data's correlations may be in the short-run, they are relatively static measures, such as observed relationships between price and choice, product location and consumer behavior, previous purchases and next purchase, "likes" and next purchase, online search activity and political preference, trips to the plate and trips to the bases, age and music downloads, etc.

The only defensible way to base strategic decisions on historical correlations is to accept the *ceteris paribus* assumption that all other things will remain equal over the long-run. Big data as a tool for looking at the future is therefore problematic. Not only does big data downplay causality; it only analyzes relationships between discrete events and behaviors at fixed points in the past. The absence of any procedures to consider events that have never before happened—one of forecasting's strengths—is also a problem. In conclusion, I think methodological limitations will prevent big data from becoming the next crystal ball, but it will continue to have considerable merit for figuring out how to do better in the present.

The Future of Big Data

Although big data is well-positioned as a tactical tool, the extent of its success over time will be significantly influenced by a few factors that have not received much attention. Leaders in the realm of big data need to be strategically responsive to these challenges in order for it to grow rather than flounder in the complex, chaotic environments where it is currently the object of so much attention.

Its very name, big data, focuses attention on the incredible volume of numbers available to be analyzed. However, the name says nothing about the quality of the numbers, and we have already seen how bad data be a big problem. GIGO—garbage in, garbage out—is a universal law. Larger data bases are not better data bases if the numbers are invalid or unreliable. Big data will not live up to its potential if improvements in analytical capabilities are not accompanied by improvements in data. Leaders in the field, therefore, need to become champions for collecting only top-quality numbers. The future of their enterprise will be determined by how well they meet this strategic goal—big good data. (Chapter 3's discussion of data quality is as relevant to big data as it is to predicting and forecasting.)

A related risk to big data's future is suggested by the common phrase, "drowning in data." Too much data is too much data, even if we have the capabilities to process all of it. The costs of collecting, storing, analyzing, and reporting information have fallen dramatically over the past two decades, but they are not free. Big data could end up costing more than it is worth, even at very low prices. Therefore, progressive leaders will work to keep marginal costs below marginal revenues all along the data chain.

The future of big data is likely to be enhanced if it becomes an academic discipline with departments and institutes of big data studies. An online search produces hundreds of references to studies of its applications in various fields (e.g., big data and medical research, big data and marketing, big data and accident prevention) but very little evidence of big data as a comprehensive, multidisciplinary field of study in itself. It would benefit from scholarly development of its own process improvement methods, return on investment (ROI) analyses, professional ethics, accreditation criteria, evaluation standards, etc. A few promising moves have been taken in this direction, but we have a lot more to learn about big data *per se*.

Last, and definitely not least, big data will need to deal directly with its problems and failures in order to thrive in the future. After several years of rave reviews, it is suddenly getting some bad press that could lead to private opposition, public regulation, and other impediments. For example, outrage over national security surveillance data could lead to general limits on big data, including individual rights to opt out of data bases and individual power to control the use of personal information and be compensated for its use. Providers of big data services could also become significantly liable for third-party losses due to theft or loss of personal data. Much work needs to be done to prevent the big data bubble from bursting.

A lot more should and will be said on all these points. I simply conclude with a forecast: big data has a high probability of survival and growth, but with storms and a few surprises along the way. Big data is very unlikely to become a good crystal ball, but it offers considerable promise as a mirror for seeing things now from a better angle.

Index

About the Author

Jeffrey C. Bauer, PhD, is an internationally recognized health futurist and medical economist. As an independent industry thought leader, he forecasts the evolution of health care and develops practical approaches to improving the medical sector of the American economy. He is widely known for his specific proposal to create an efficient and effective health care delivery system through multistakeholder partnerships and other initiatives focused in the private sector.

Dr. Bauer has published more than 250 articles, books, web pages, and videos on health care delivery. He speaks frequently to national and international audiences about key trends in health care, medical science, technology, information systems, reimbursement, public policy, and creative problem solving. Dr. Bauer is quoted often in the national press and writes regularly for professional journals that cover the business of health care. He is the author of *Statistical Analysis for Health Care Decision-Makers* and coauthor of *Paradox and Imperatives in Health Care: How Efficiency, Effectiveness, and E-Transformation Can Conquer Waste and Optimize Quality,* both published by CRC Press.

As a consultant, he has assisted hundreds of providers, purchasers, and payer organizations with strategic planning and performance improvement. He served in several major corporate positions from 1999 to 2010, including vice president for health care forecasting and strategy for ACS, a Xerox company.

His previous consulting firm, The Bauer Group, specialized in consumer-focused strategic planning and development of clinical affiliation agreements for multihospital networks from 1984 to 1992.

In his academic career, Dr. Bauer was a full-time teacher and administrator at the University of Colorado Health Sciences Center in Denver from 1973 to 1984, where he held appointments as associate professor and as assistant chancellor for planning and program development. He also served concurrently for four years as health policy advisor to Colorado Governor Richard D. Lamm. From 1992 to 1998, Dr. Bauer was a visiting professor in administrative medicine at the Medical School of the University of Wisconsin–Madison, where he taught physician leaders how to conduct research and evaluate published studies.

He received his PhD in economics from the University of Colorado–Boulder. He graduated from Colorado College in Colorado Springs with a BA in economics and completed a

Figure 0.1   Jeff Bauer working at a Doppler weather radar console (National Center for Atmospheric Research Hail Studies Project. New Raymer, Colorado. Summer, 1968).

certificate in political studies at the University of Paris (France). During his academic career, he was a Boettcher Scholar, a Ford Foundation Independent Scholar, a Fulbright Scholar (Switzerland), and a Kellogg Foundation National Fellow. Dr. Bauer lives in Chicago, where he is actively involved in painting and music.

For Product Safety Concerns and Information please contact our EU
representative GPSR@taylorandfrancis.com
Taylor & Francis Verlag GmbH, Kaufingerstraße 24, 80331 München, Germany